Ambient Echoes
A
REFLECTION OF THE CLASSIC SPANKING/POEMS EXPRESSIONS CONFESSIONS

By

CLEO C. CONEY JR.

© 2002 by CLEO C. CONEY JR. All rights reserved.

No part of this book may be reproduced, stored in a retrieval system, or transmitted by any means, electronic, mechanical, photocopying, recording, or otherwise, without written permission from the author.

ISBN: 1-4033-0916-7 (e-book)
ISBN: 1-4033-0917-5 (Softcover)
ISBN: 1-4033-0918-3 (Hardcover)

Library of Congress Control Number: 2002108025

This book is printed on acid free paper.

Printed in the United States of America
Bloomington, IN

1st Books - rev. 06/17/02

MY INSPIRATION

My inspiration for this booklet comes from all the children that continue to need guidance. This booklet is dedicated to my parents Annie R. Coney and Cleo C. Coney Sr.

My hope is that in these pages you will find memories of your childhood that make you smile. Respect discipline and you will earn respect.

Any perceived slights against people or organizations are unintentional. Although the author experienced the contents of this booklet first hand, the author does not authorize, or advise, or suggest, or condone physical action upon children. The author does not claim to be an expert, or an authority in child behavior modification. This work is strictly for entertainment purposes only. Please seek professional child counseling when dealing with concerns of your own family.

JUST A WORD

A child was born to a military family in the mid sixties, nineteen sixty-four to be exact. Not just any child, but a black male child born the last of four children to Cleo and Annie Coney. This young man had parents that recognized God and family as important values to never be forgotten. The family group would be his guide to ethics, behavior, and manners. I was that young black child. Named after my father, by my father, while my mother was unconscious after giving birth to me. The story goes that my mother had another name selected for the baby. Fathers however, make decisions when mothers are unable to, which is why I became a junior. Now when it came to child behavior, my parents didn't play, they were serious folks who made it job number one in the raising of my siblings and I to respectable adults. I look back on those days now with a special wonderment. The next pages contain stories and lessons my sore butt recalls being dealt out.

Cleo C. Coney Jr.

THE GIFTS

GIFT ONE: THE TRADITIONAL BLACK FAMILY xi

GIFT TWO: IN THE MIX, OR IN THE VICINITY BUTT WHOOPINGS xviii

GIFT THREE: YOUR MOMMA CAN STILL HEAR YOU xxiii

GIFT FOUR: PROMISES NOT THREATS xxviii

GIFT FIVE: GET YOUR BEHIND TORE UP xxxiii

GIFT SIX: ACTING A FOOL AND CLOWNING xxxviii

GIFT SEVEN: DON'T LET THE STREET LIGHTS CATCH YOU liii

GIFT EIGHT: CANCEL CHRISTMAS lvi

GIFT NINE: MOMMA DIDN'T PLAY THAT lx

GIFT TEN: MY BUTT LIVE THROUGH IT lxiv

THE TRADITIONAL BLACK FAMILY

As a child growing up in a black family in America with traditional black family values, a butt whooping was the end result of the lack of following parental instructions. A butt whooping could also be the end result of the child (myself), making a poor decision based on what other kids my age, that I had come into contact with were allowed to do or behave. In many instances a butt whooping would seem to develop out of an improper body movement, perhaps a facial expression, or walk, that may have been misconstrued as deliberate disrespect. Sometimes a butt whooping would come it seemed out of nowhere! But later on in life a majority of past butt whoopings thought of earlier as misdirected (By my behind), where in fact very valuable lessons, that today have calmly kept my siblings and I on the straight and narrow.

Anytime, anyplace, anywhere, with anything, those were the ass whooping prime directives. Hopefully, I would never receive an ass whooping in front of my peers, or relatives. But as I can recall some grand butt whoopings, (From grandparents) there are none more escalating or embarrassing! The reason for that is, if grandma had to whoop your butt, then daddy's going to whoop your butt for putting grandma through a hassle, and momma's going to whoop your behind for embarrassing your father in front of his mother! Heads up, ears and eyes open, respect and good manners seem to always prevent seventy five percent of all butt whoopings. The other twenty five percent...well, something's just cause a butt whooping. The following are a few that I seem to remember quite well that would lead to a butt whooping in my family. (By no means did I commit all of these by myself, how bout it sibs?)

1. Any grade below a C, and sometimes an A depending on the class.

2. Any call to a parent from teacher about poor behavior in class, or study habits.

3. Any loud or unruly behavior that included running through the house. (You run outside the house.)

4. Being in the vicinity of someplace or someone where a crime was committed. (You should know better.)

5. Forgetting to do part or all of an assigned chore.

6. Questioning parental authority. (I brought you in this world; I'll take you out.)

7. Lying.

8. Doing anything with out parental permission that required supervision.

9. Allowing any friends or playmates to disrespect your home.

10. Unauthorized eating of any special desert. (Cakes, Pies, etc.)

First of all, at no time was my behind safe from being whooped. My parents owned my butt, and I didn't take ownership of my butt until they said I did. Even today ownership is in occasional dispute. Butt whoopings weren't just from family members, but also from so called concerned adults outside of your immediate family. This list includes people like your neighbors. You see your neighbors had an unannounced pact with your parental committee. This pact allowed them to correct your incorrectness in your parent's immediate absence, for the benefit of your own good. (A butt whooping) I still believe today that they just wanted to whoop the behinds of other people's kids, and on some occasions so do I. Which brings me to this, my butt whooping experiences have given me a wealth of knowledge and wisdom in the development of human character. After all, I've witnessed first hand how children have developed with parents who refused to correct their children. These kids have grown up to be disrespecting rude adults, disrespecting everyone they come in contact with. My belief is that they didn't learn from example and lesson. Some parents teach bad lessons and give poor examples. Unfortunately in those instances children may not learn the importance of getting along with others. It's a basic behavior requirement, which makes co-existing with other people in society obtainable. There are a lot of people in America who never learned this lesson. But enough about these types already, I mean, I run into kids in public places all the time with the type of behavior that would of earned them a Guinness book of records butt whooping in my mother's home! CNN would do an in depth look, into the butt whooping, the television anchor would say something like, "it's Day one hundred fifty three of the butt whooping of the century". Now a butt whooping is not always the correct method for handling misbehavior.

Although the threat of an occasional butt whooping that is carried out swiftly, and directly as promised by the parent is a very effective form of " I ain't going to raise no bad ass kids maintenance". (See my family)

My parents never let us go hungry, never locked us into small spaces, put us into boiling oil, or burned us with anything. That would be child abuse. But a good hot butt whooping is not child abuse if it is connected to a previous warning, directed towards behavior modification, and carried out as promised consistently, from day one. You don't let your child become a problem child, or some punk majoring in crime and then try to modify the behavior. You start with stories and examples, which show the positives and negatives of actions; this is how I remember it being among the black families I grew up with. Today, I see young adults bringing about butt whoopings from avoidable life situations. As an adult I know how hard it must be to get a butt whooping from life. Learning lessons later on in life is always harder, and could come with dire consequences verses learning earlier in life. Hopefully you had parents like mine that made sure that my siblings and I caught the butt whooping boat early.

Life is about choices, early in my life I had choices, some could lead to happiness, others could lead to a butt whooping. This "correct choice" lesson I found worked for me in ninety nine percent of all possible scenarios. Good grades meant I studied hard, while studying I learned, if I learned enough I advanced, if I advanced far enough I would graduate. Hopefully after graduating I would qualify for college and graduating from college would provide the opportunity to obtain a higher paying job. Hopefully, a higher paying job would lead to some sort of stability, which would help provide for my future family. On the other hand a bad grade lead to a butt whooping, and if you didn't straightened up you're act, then you had to go. Harder times would be ahead and so forth, and so forth. Some how not getting my behind whooped always seemed to be the best option for me. The thing about yesterdays butt spankings is that they were only half of what my parents would of received from their parents. I wonder what kind of butt whooping is going on today around the country with all these students carrying guns to school? One thing is constant though and that's an adult butt whooping. There are quite a few young adults learning that lesson today. We all know of instances in our own cities of a much-publicized butt whooping. Some of these butt whoopings took place because on a particular occasion someone was in the wrong place at the wrong time. My mother would say, "

Shouldn't have been there in the first place". Some of these butt whoopings are kind of funny, and others have been out right tragic. But we can all agree that it's much more comfortable when it's not us that opened that can of ass whooping. The following pages reflect instances in my life that would of brought about a butt whooping, and some did.

Please do not hold me responsible if you decide to act up with your folks and they decide to beat your behind! I am not responsible for your butt, or the whooping your behind could quite possible receive. Remember, while reading this that these were the good old days with no guns in schools, or drugs running through and devastating entire neighborhoods. If you're my age, I bet your butt can still feel that last whooping!

IN THE MIX, OR IN THE VICINITY BUTT WHOOPINGS

Out of all the possible butt whoopings you could possible get, in the mix or in the vicinity butt whoopings were the most frustrating. After all, you didn't really do anything and you didn't act on anything, but you were just too close to the happening in question. The end result in ninety nine percent of the instances was a butt whooping. These spankings were coupled with conversation during the actual whooping, basically one-sided. For example, the parent might say, "What were you doing with those bad boys?" You'd answer like normal, Um, Ah, Ouch! Um, Ah, Ouch! Oooouch! Oooouch! Oooouch! Followed by the parent saying something like, "Shut up when I'm talking to you!!" Each swing of the whooping device (usually the closes belt, switch, or extension cord) just what ever would tighten your butt up with the quickness, delivered in time with the one-sided conversation in a rhythmic flow married to the parents speech infliction. What your parents were actually helping to prepare you for was the development of your decision-making ability, which was based on probability. If you play with kids from group A, what might happen? What is their play history? Will they find a way to get into trouble? Yes! Will your behind get in trouble? Yes! So the in the mix or in the vicinity butt whoopings were very important, of course at the time they seemed unfair, with out merit, frustrating, and at times with out warning. Then there were the times that some knick-knack or furniture came up broken. God please, don't let a piece of crystal or vase come up broken! And for goodness sake, don't be the only one in the room when it was discovered. For your behinds sake, it wouldn't be wise to be the last one who had been seen in the vicinity of the room, why you ask? Well because that's a guaranteed butt whooping. Who ate some of the cake? Sometimes none of the siblings could quite answer that question. Well then, that's a group in the mix butt whooping! Oh, and ya'll wake Cleo up so he can get his too. (Parent) The neighbor said they saw you near the fence when his back yard caught on fire. (Child) I was watching what those kids you told me not to play with were doing, and I was on our side of the fence. (Parent) So you watched them set the neighbors yard on fire, and you didn't tell anybody did you? You should have told someone because the fire could of come over into our yard and burned down our damn house! The end result would be an in the mix or in the vicinity butt whooping. You see, an in the mix or in the vicinity butt whooping is the parents preventive maintenance education. Helping to bring about the growth of the reasoning portion of the child's brain. Teaches thinking before acting, or getting even semi-involved in any scenario in question. You see, in a black family, not even an alien abduction can get you out of a butt whooping! For starters, you shouldn't have been in a place that aliens frequent. You already know that they abduct people. You watch television stupid! Plus you shouldn't have done what ever you did to provoke them into abducting your behind anyway! So you're going to get an in the vicinity butt whooping, might as well get ready for it. Now while growing up, there was always a kid that you wanted to play with that did things that your parents looked down on. He or she was the kid that had way cool toys, but they were also the kid that talked back to their parents. The kid would say things like "No!" or "You shut up!" and the parents would say things back like, "That's no way to talk", or "Shush your trash mouth". The classic slack parent would respond with " If you want to talk like that then go outside". I would trip off of this kid's so called parents, because in our home I knew that kid would never ever finish a sentence or disrespect his folks. That kids behind would be completely tore up! My folks didn't play that. But because of those cool toys, you'd find a way to play with this kid. Then one day while playing with the kid that your parents told you not to play with, something happened. Now you weren't at the exact spot were the happening took place, but you knew you'd have to explain where you were, and whom you were with at the time. Lying would not save your behind, it would only secure additional pain in the form of a more concentrated butt whooping to prevent future lying. Before telling your parents what went on, the thing to do would be to bequeath your toys and play stuff to the appropriate siblings. The in the mix or in the vicinity butt whooping would be coming ashore on your butt like a category five hurricane. You also knew in the back of your head that you had let your folks down, after all, if you had kept to their wishes this could have all been avoided. Can we get this whooping over with please? (I'll never do it again momma, I promise...Mmmmm Hmmmm)

    I truly believe that an in the mix or in the vicinity butt whooping can keep a growing child out of a lot of trouble. The capsulization of an entire thought process to include possible out comes of possible actions, expands the mind at an early age. Would I ever play with that kid again? Hell no! Finding things to do with out playing with the wrong kids, or going somewhere I wasn't supposed to be was not difficult at all.

I could always play with siblings, draw, write a poem, or play with the dog. Oh, you can bet I'd find something to do. It was all-fine and dandy with me, because being the youngest I had the softest butt, and I was tired of getting my behind caught up in the mix, or in the vicinity of another ass whooping.

YOUR MOMMA CAN STILL HEAR YOU

So many times I remember getting my behind tore up because I forgot the golden rule, "Your momma can still hear you fool!" Let's set the scene, I'm in the back yard lighting matches into the barbecue grill, not that were planning to cook out on this particular day, but I'm just lighting matches, for fun and tossing them into the grill. Now my momma looks at me through the kitchen window and says, "Stop playing with those matches Cleo". I respond with, "yes momma". Ceasing my activity with the matches I just look in the grille a moment and then turn away, as I begin walking I say to myself softly, " Nothing wrong with lighting matches in the grill, she's so picky. Now I'm a good twenty-five feet from the kitchen window when I'm mumbling softly to myself, when I hear, "come here boy and bring a switch so I can show you just how picky I can be with your legs!" But that doesn't fully represent her hearing abilities that led to many a butt whooping. Eighty percent of the time she over heard my behind inside of the house, mumbling real low in response to some parental direction. I remember many times a butt whooping would just be floating in the air looking for a behind to land on. Mainly during those quite times when you know something is heavy on momma's mind. Those were the times when you made sure to complete every task she asked you. However, my second to oldest sister hadn't completed a chore once, and she was walking away from my mother to complete the task and softly said "Dawg!" in response to the parental direction that seemed unjust in the mind of a child. My mother's response was, "I heard that, now bring me a belt so I can give you something to be dawged about". I think I went into the back yard, just in case there was an errant blow from the belt while she and my sister danced the butt whooping dance about the house, just my mom, my sister, and the belt. Wow! What timing. You see, even though she was older, at the moment of her softly spoken remarks, she too had forgotten the golden rule, " Your momma can still hear you. There were times I was asked on different occasions to stop playing with my toys, it's time to eat, or it's time to go to bed by my mother. During those times she usually yelled across the house at least two rooms away. I'd respond like always, "yes momma". Five minutes later my butt was being tore up because she could still hear me playing, even though I believed that I took extra steps in being quiet. Not even under the covers with a flashlight to finish reading my HULK comic book was I safe. She heard me turning pages through the covers, down the hall; turn right into the living room, and through the sounds of the television.

I'd hear her coming and would play possum, but she'd tear my behind up anyway! She'd say something like; " I got something for that possum behind of yours!" I can hear you turning pages in here son! You do what I ask you when I ask you too! Not when you want to! Now give me that book. Yes momma. There could even be a big family reunion going on with the house full of people making noise, and my momma could still hear any response, mumble, talk back, or sigh from a hundred yards away, and that would be your behind! Oh and please, don't be on the phone too long! Momma would pick up the other extension and say, " tell your friend bye now!" or if she'd told me to get off two minutes previously and I mumble something to my friend on the other end of the phone like "she's all over me I got to go", from the kitchen she'd say hurry up and hang up, because now I'm going to be all over your butt! Once again foolishly forgetting the golden rule, " Your momma can still hear you". I've been contemplating running a series of audio test with mothers of different ages and comparing the same test to women with no children. I'm almost certain that mothers have a greater sensitivity to tones and frequencies in the" <u>under your breath ranges</u>." Growing up was frustrating at times, I mean, I'd find myself checking for hidden microphones all the time. It wasn't always an under your breath word or phrase that would trigger the butt whooping either. In a whole group of instances an audible expression of air through one's nose or mouth would not only trigger a butt whooping from my mother, but from my father as well. "I'll give you something to be huffy and puffy about", they'd say. Try me with your young behind if you want to, but a smart man wouldn't bet on it. How fortunate my sisters and I were to have parents who loved us enough to care about what kind of adult citizens and examples we would become. It's easy for passive parents to just write their children off and say, " Oh, their just bad kids", or "I just don't know what to do with these kids". But my parents know that children need more than food, shelter, and praise. Children also need positive examples, lessons of respect, patience, and priorities. If my sisters and I had never learned these positive lessons, we'd be different citizens today. Our parents never tolerated any disgust or unwilling attitudes even in the smallest examples.

Bring your behind here! We don't play that. Just try and talk back to my mother while she's four rooms away, or even inside the house while you're on the outside of the house. That my friend will be your behind! Because she will always be able to hear my siblings and I, no matter how old we get. We must always respect our mother and father, and keep our mouths shut despite the temptation to do otherwise. A child must learn to accept their current position until their old enough to be held accountable for their actions and control their own fate. We owe our existence to our folks after all. Until that day, keep your mouth shut and remember the golden rule.

PROMISES NOT THREATS

You can believe it when I tell you that my mother and father made promises and not threats. They always carried out every promise …involving tearing up your butt if you didn't follow through with their wishes.

There was no," Didn't I tell you" more than once. Now these wishes of theirs were things like good behavior on the part of the child, chores, correct speech, proper posture, school grades, eating habits, and the world famous sibling fighting! My folks basically didn't take or accept any crap! What worried me more than the promise my folks would make to us kids, was the thought of someone crossing my mother.

They wouldn't know what hit them if Ann Coney's wrong buttons were pushed! I would have these day mares of my mother being lead away by special forces troops after she leveled a town where some unknowing person either threatened her children, husband, or her personal well being. I knew that the Native American and African blood combination flowing through her veins was nothing to mess with when boiling! This strong black woman who picked cotton, corn, and what ever else needed to be done growing up on a Georgia farm, had a grip that was for real. You didn't ever want to make the mistake of mistreating one of her offspring. I have no doubt that my mother could have, and would have taken anyone out with the quickness, who had done anything wrong to one of her children. As Mr. "T" used to say, "I pity the fool", that would make that huge error. However, my siblings and myself bore witness first hand on what a promise is and what a threat is, so let's go on. When my folks said, " Cleo, if you do that again I'm going to tear your behind up", that was a promise. This was sure to be true because not once had my folks ever strayed from what they said they'd do. If they hadn't ever carried out what they said they'd do, then those statements would of been nothing more than idle threats. Over a period of time as a child I would of known that they didn't mean what they said, and I would of just done what ever, and acted like it's a game not to do what they had asked of me. I've always felt that there was nothing cute about not doing what my parents said. They never laughed and neither did my butt when it came to serious parental guidance. All kids try everything at least once, at some level of testing a parent's level of authority, and flexing their own perceived independence. (You have none until your butt is out of the house.) The most dangerous word to use with my folks was "why". You never ask why when your mother and father have laid out the law. Period. You ask why when talking about nature, mathematics, literature, art, space travel, auto racing, cereal box graphics, street signs, television programs etc., but you never, ever ask why to a chore, lesson, or a direction from parent to child involving behavioral modification. YOU ALREADY KNOW WHY? Because your behind did it, or your butt messed up, or your butt didn't follow direction, or your butt is asking for more! You did what your parents asked you to do out of respect, out of love, out of the fact that your butt is under their roof until you can afford to live on your own, even then you don't ask why, because lighting might hit you. Even in biblical sense children are to obey their parents or live short lives. That's enough for me and I'm not the religious type...but do you really want to take that chance? I can remember legitimately forgetting a chore, and all of a sudden I was caught up in a butt whooping, outside in the front yard in front of the neighbors, and who ever else was out there. I mean that butt whooping crept up on me like chemical warfare! After that first stroke of the belt I remembered every chore I needed to do for the next ten years. It was like a cloud had been lifted from off my head.

Oh yeah, yeah, that's it! The garage Cleo, clean out the garage! Now that I look back on those spankings I can clearly see how they could of been avoided. Obviously my folks let me know up front that they would tear my butt up if I didn't comply with the set parameters. But like most young kids, and teenagers, listening skills weren't at the level that they should be. There's so much to do and see that matters in the short-lived existence called youth. (Or so they believe) It's easy to get caught up in the mix, wait a minute, being in the mix could get my butt whooped.

Sometimes I wonder if it was just an era that my folks were from that blessed the almighty ass whooping.

I remember the day my aunt Frances, God Bless her soul, tore my cousin Andre's butt up at the dinner table! Andre and I had been watching the Saturday afternoon creature feature movie "Godzilla vs. King Kong", over at my aunt's house, when she expressed that we eat all of our food that she had prepared for us. Once at the table I quickly ate everything, Andre ate everything except his vegetables. My aunt Frances came in and looked at our plates, she said she was going to tear Andre's butt up if he didn't eat his vegetables. Now, Andre must of started day dreaming, or his mind had some how turned to jelly contemplating the vegetables in his plate. He was looking at them; they were looking back at him. In a matter of minutes my aunt Frances returned to the dinning room with a belt, and caught Andre with out his shirt on, at the table with all his vegetables still on his plate! (The fact that he had extra exposed flesh would count against him shortly.) Feeling the tension in the air, and having previous experience with black mothers who didn't play, I wisely sought shelter.

As I had predicted, Andre got his butt tore up, along with his chest, shoulders, and back, by the way Andre ate all his vegetables. The latter aunt Frances instance was a perfect example of a promise not a threat. My aunt Frances who isn't with us now, graduated from the same ass whooping school as my parents did. They didn't play. It's funny just how funny those memories are now, but at the time it was so scary. You learned to listen hard to protect your behind from the promise's not threats from your folks, or relatives who were in positions that allowed the correcting of your butt through the standard "Tear that behind up" procedures.

GET YOUR BEHIND TORE UP

Oh yeah, I've heard it many times from different parents and relatives. Please understand that this statement wasn't always directed at me. Let's straighten that out first. It's just a statement that was a warning sign of the possible butt whooping to come. What held my interest in this awkward statement was not the actual threat, or even the heart wrenching panic that occasionally set in, but the visualizing of the statement verbatim. I mean let's face it; if you actually tore a butt up it would be a mess. Where did this statement come from? Although it was a scary thought to have your butt tore up by a belt or switch, the statement was one of my favorite butt whooping phrases that are stored ever so carefully in a special section of my mind. Also in that special section are other memorable phrases that described butt whoopings that I had been threaten with, or over heard at a butt whooping location other than my folks address. I remember that my uncle liked to say, "dressed him down". This was another interesting phrase, as long as it wasn't directed towards me. My Uncle would be in a conversation with my father, or one of my aunt's and he'd say, "Yep Frankie dressed him down". This meant either my cousin

Ramon or his little brother Bruce would of gotten "Dressed Down". Which was just basically an ass whooping from my aunt Frankie. God bless her soul, she's whom I learned to successfully land big fish from, using inexpensive fishing outfits. Of course if at anytime I didn't follow her wishes, she'd quickly dress me down to correct my behavior, which was for my own safety near the water. Picture a group of young children wading out into the shallows of the Gulf of Mexico, off the beaches of Fort De Soto, in St. Petersburg Florida. Every kid holding a cane pole with about seven to twelve feet of fishing line on the end, a couple of split shot weights a hook and a live shrimp on the end. Only one adult watching over us all, and that was my aunt Frankie. So when and if we needed to be dressed down, (a butt whooping) it would be to set an example for the whole group of kids. But as I remember the threat of a butt whooping was all we needed to remain focused on the fishing at hand. Another statement along the lines of "Get your behind tore up", and "Dress'em Down", was the phrase "Tighten you up", or the cult favorite " Tighten your ass up". This would fascinate my very active young mind because the concept of tightening for me would be like the action of turning a bolt, or lacing something until it was taught. But after severe brainstorming, I assume it means that the child is acting to loosely, or "clowning", which we'll examine in the next chapter. My father once told me that if I didn't start acting right soon, he'd tighten my ass right up! There was no question what so ever as to what he meant. My father was going to beat my behind, so that I would straighten up, or tighten up as it were. My folks didn't really say, "Do you want a Spanking?" they may have but I don't ever remember them saying anything so soft. They'd say I'm going to teach you a lesson in a minute because you're about to get your behind tore up! meaning, "Dressed Down", which meant getting my butt "Tightened Up", all in all an "ass whooping". Now they might get smooth on occasion and say something like, "I got what you need in this belt", or "I need to help you with your listening", and the frequently used, "Your mouths writing a check that your butt can't cash". How can we forget, "You're about to open a can full of ass whooping!" All of the above statements meant that a butt whooping was on its way, first class, special delivery straight to my behind! Get your behind tore up was and is an interesting statement. When you consider child behavior modification, the statement is pretty direct and will quickly quiet a room full of black children. You'll see them look around to verify that it's not their own butt that's going to get tore up. The kids are also checking to make sure their behinds aren't in the mix or in the vicinity of the kid whose about to get his or hers butt tore up! Sometimes I'd find myself with a group of friends or relatives all playing loudly in a room, and my father might interrupt...for the second time and say, "Who wants to get their butts tore up?" Well, we'd be pretty quiet after that. The group of kids would just be looking at each other with big sad eyes. Somebody would say, "Well what do ya'll want to play now?" Hey you idiot, the playing is over man! Whenever I'd get my butt tore up there was one thing that really bothered me. It was the knowledge that my father was sure to bring up this butt whooping again in the future as a reference to a current situation. For example, my father might say, "Cleo, You know you got your behind tore up last time you messed up some new school clothes, so you better watch it this time and use your head. This would totally drain any excitement or fun thoughts from the event that I had planned on attending. Why, why? Did he have to bring up a past butt whooping in front of a girl? Of all the embarrassing statements why would he say something like, " I remember when Cleo was still doing his business in his drawers, or I remember the time Cleo got his behind tore up real good. It's just a good warm, parental story to mark a time period in the life of his son. Come on Daddy! Now don't you get huffy with me son, after all, we gave you your little money to go out with and you can still get your butt tore up! Damn Demoralizing. But at least they were just being friendly with my date. I mean I was the one trying to rush out of the house right? Well ah, at that low point it didn't really matter if they "Tore my behind up", dressed me down", or Tightened my ass up". I had already sunk down to the depths of shame where only giant squid live. Get your behind tore up, the phrase that shall always be with me and my siblings, and probably you too. That is, if you had parents like mine that didn't play.

Momma and Daddy and Kindra at Florida Home

Momma and Daddy

From left to right:
Chandra, Andrea, Kindra and in front Cleo Jr.

Cleo Jr.

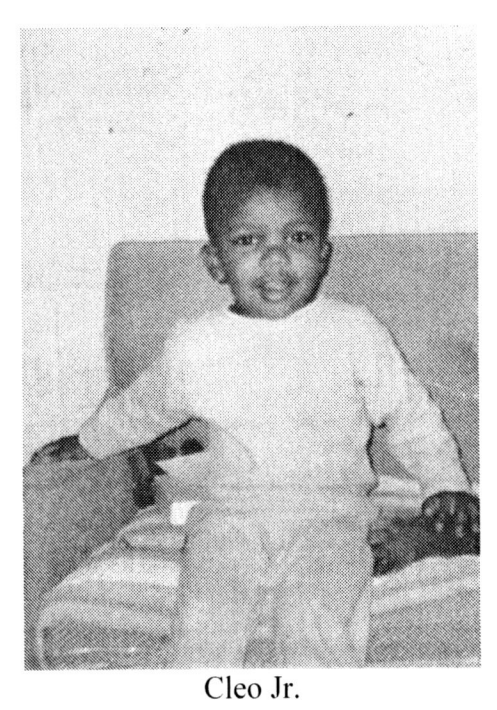

Daddy and Momma

Kindra

Daddy in Alaska the younger version

Andrea as a baby

Chandra Momma and Andrea on a passport photo

Chandra

Momma the younger version

ACTING A FOOL AND CLOWNING

Acting a fool and clowning, my youngest sister Kindra had this down one hundred percent!!!

You can ask any of my closest relatives who've witnessed first hand the type of clowning and acting a fool that would make Jerry Lewis and the Three Stooges Proud. The Queen of aggravation, my sweet sister Kindra's acting a fool and clowning brought about many a butt whooping. Now, she wasn't the only one clowning in the family, she was just the most well known of all the family clowns. During infrequent visits to our home, my cousin Frenda from Pompano Beach would get into the act and escalate the clowning. This behavior aggravated everyone in the house including my folks, who would let them continue until the butt whooping was let loose like a hunting dog on a rabbit. My sister Kindra liked to focus her best efforts on her favorite target, me! Let's start with the pencils in the nose while I'm still asleep, I wonder if she remembers the dart into the knee, or the surprise weekly choke hold from behind, while sitting on the couch watching television. None of my family can forget any of her Pratt falls, like tripping through the living room furniture while my Parents entertained guest. This crazy sister of mine would sometimes come into a room where I was at, and begin to sing as loud and as irritating as possible. She'd do all of this while sliding across the floor in socks, pajamas, and uncombed hair. She would also like to blow her nose in tissue, and then try to hand them to you. AAHHH!! GET AWAY!! You get the picture. Well, since I was her favorite target, she would continue her attacks on my senses until I would chase her through the house while she yelled at the top of her young lungs, daddy! daddy! Cleo's chasing me! This only made me angrier because she started the whole escapade. My father would appear and say, " Don't hit your sisters". I'd be so frustrated that I would just go outside and ride my bike as fast as I could. To picture her hiding behind my father makes me laugh hysterically now, but at the same time I still have a little residual urge to go ride a bike. My mom liked to say, "Stop all that clowning around before I have to tear something up". Don't run in this house, you hear me? We'd both answer, " yes, momma". Half hour later my sister and I were getting our behinds tore up for running in the house. There were other instances that represent clowning that I remember, but Kindra's clowning antics just take the cake! My sisters and I were all very good at interacting together, from playing post office, to those stupid family board games, and skits. So I guess you could say we were a normal family. (Sometimes I wonder?) One day during an extended bout of clowning by my sister Kindra, which would usually start by her coming into my room and removing the covers from my feet in the morning. We got into it real good. Kindra would get some good punches in on me and then take off running for my father. Now on this Saturday morning I was running a tad faster than normal. I ran her down and caught her square in her back with a good lick of my fist before she could reach my father. Surprised by the blow to the back, she immediately did a one hundred and eighty degree turn and took off after me.

    I ran through the living room into the hallway leading to the den. I turned into the den and slammed the door shut behind me without looking back. (Laughing all the way) Kindra, who was chasing me couldn't slow down in time; I mean that's how close she was to nabbing me. She ran smack into the door, BOOM! at full speed. There was a moment of silence with only the faint sounds of a distant lawn mower down the street creeping in underneath the door. The next sound was a casual knock at the door. I ever so carefully opened the door slowly so as to not allow her to bum rush me if it was her who knocked. I couldn't believe what I saw. There my sister stood with the biggest knot I'd ever seen outside of a cartoon, right on her upper forehead. I knew instantly that her head had tested the density of the door moments earlier right on that spot. She looked at me with big sad eyes and said, "I'm telling daddy". (Oh, Oh) My father whooped both our behinds for acting a fool and clowning in the house. He made us sit on the floor apart from each other in the room where he sat watching television. Each time I would look over at my sister, my eyes still swollen and teary, she would remove the ice pack from her head revealing the big knot on her forehead for me to see. I felt ripped off! The day I get a good lick in on her, and she has to bust her head on the door chasing me. Well, my daddy did say for me not to hit my sister's. I should've listened, but noooooooo! I had to get my butt tore up. Acting a fool and clowning was a phrase used widely to describe the behavior of the kids in our house, and sometimes the kids of my parent's friends. I enjoyed the phrase when my father used it to comment on the nightly news. I remember a news story on the releasing of the bulls in Spain. The story used some footage of some unlucky runners getting trampled by a huge bull. My father said,

"Look at them clowns Cleo". Now that's what you get when you act a fool and want to clown around an angry bull on the loose.

Sometimes while the family watched Soul Train to check out the latest dances, my father would say, " That's not even dancing, just waving their arms around like fools and clowning. One day we were watching a nature program on ocean predators, when they showed some footage of divers getting attacked by great white sharks. I knew what my father was going to say before he even said it. Do you see these fools Cleo, clowning around some great white sharks with chum in the water. That's what you get when you act a fool and start clowning around some hungry sharks! Cleo, change the channel I don't want to see these clowns anymore. Isn't there a good war picture on? Now the same thing was said to the kids at times about their current activities. We didn't have to be doing anything dangerous or uncommon. The funny thing was though, the majority of the time my folks were right. Like the time I was hanging upside down from the grapefruit tree swinging back and forth. My father said, Ok, act a fool if you want to, but that clowning around is going to catch up to your butt one day. And it did. I fell upside down on my head a few days later.

There was even a time I was wrestling with some of the neighborhood boys out in the front yard, and my daddy said, ya'll need to stop clowning around in that grass, it will have ya'll itching and somebody might get hurt. He was right again. Lucky for me though, this particular occasion didn't develop into a butt whooping. Now, um, a week Later...

DON'T LET THE STREET LIGHTS CATCH YOU

As I got older my parents allowed me further liberties as they saw fit. You worked your way up from don't leave the yard, to, don't go further than next door, to, don't go off the street, to, don't leave the neighborhood, and then be home before the street lights come on. This last liberty was like a blessing because that meant I was able to check out some of my schoolmates several streets over. We gathered in a neighborhood group and played war, football, kill the carrier, baseball, and smash ball and rode our bikes to the Quickie mart for refreshments. Then there were those times when it was just too darn hot to play ball and we met in my friend Tyrone's garage and listened to tunes. When it cooled off we'd play football in the field against the guys from across the tracks. It always seemed that the games only got good right around the last fifteen or so minutes before the streetlights came on. This was a dilemma for about six of us because we lived the furthest away, and that meant high tailing it down the street to beat the streetlights arrival. Sometimes I felt like I was running for my life. If I felt I was going to be a few seconds late, I might jump our back yard fence and get the dogs to bark and chase me as if I had been in the backyard a while. My butt will attest that this didn't always work out the way I had planned. Neighbors who would be out in the evening watering their lawns would tell you what you already knew as you ran by them on your way home, "Better run fast, them street lights are about to come on". Sometimes you'd get home early and still get a butt whooping for cutting it to close. This form of behavioral modification was preparing us kids for the real world. One that is cut throat, and plays by it's own rules. You'd learn to be on time, besides it wasn't safe for a person at your age to be out after dark with out parental supervision. What do you need to be out late for anyway? You could sometimes see several young teens running into their yards at dusk from all directions. The task at hand would be to beat the flickering of the streetlights home. A wide-angle camera would've caught several butt whoopings going on simultaneously, what a snap shot! You won't see that today, if several parents beat their kids outside all the news teams would be on the street to interview the whooper's, the whooped, and the about to be whooped. Plus, the HRS would want to step in take kids, and press child abuse charges. Today, we are constantly giving young adults excuses for their bad behavior, and punishing the parents for it. Violence in every form of media you can think of, from prime time cartoons, to the nightly news, to the silver screen. But how many butts are being tore up because of bad behavior today? Not many I bet. Let's institute a nationwide street light curfew for the under eighteen crowd and see how much crime they get involved in then. Getting my butt home before the streetlights came on, boy that was something. I respect my parents more every day I live for what they instilled in me. You know those butt spankings molded me, and shaped my character. They made me a better person today then I would have been with out them. To think of the time I spent contemplating how I could keep those streetlights from coming on. I never ever thought about the fact that I would need to hold up the sun too, since they were light sensitive.

CANCEL CHRISTMAS

There are some things that parents can do to children, that can whoop their behinds just as hard as a belt, but with out making physical contact. As a parent you have to decide in a split second which behavior modification tactic is best and the most efficient. There are seasonal phrases that can have an immediate effect on the child's behavior, listed below are some of the strongest phrases.

1.) That's it! Everybody out of the pool!

2.) OK then, no ice cream for you!

3.) You stay here, while the rest of the family goes to Disney World.

4.) Looks like were going to have to cancel Christmas.

Extreme caution has to be taken when using these and other behavioral modification phrases, and they can't be used so frequently that the child realizes you're bluffing. In our family the threat of a canceled Christmas loomed like a northwestern redwood shadow. Actions from other family members could trigger a possible cancellation announcement. "Well, since your big sister isn't coming home this year,"...or since your cousin's forth removed brothers, uncle, sister's, friends, children's, neighbors are making an unauthorized visit, we'll have too...But if you had something to do with knocking over the Christmas tree, or letting the dog chew up presents, or opening the oven causing the Christmas cake to fall, or blowing out the Christmas bulbs, my mother would put on that cancel Christmas face that everyone recognized. Anyone making a holiday visit would immediately be drained of the spirit upon entering the house. "Oh, I see ya'll canceled Christmas this year". The siblings and I would be mulling around all depressed and make the cancellation confession, so and so knocked over the tree, momma tore our behinds up, and now Christmas is canceled. We weren't intentionally trying to get a holiday butt whooping, we were just running through the house like momma asked us not too do. From two to three months out from Christmas, my mother and father would begin making a stash of gifts in various places around the house. Any attempt at gift espionage could result in a cancellation of Christmas. My mother, who has the hearing that would make hi tech gulf war weapons obsolete, could hear me trying to pry open that special closet. CLEO! Bring me a belt, and your butt here right now! In the back of your mind you were praying that this butt whooping you were about to receive, wasn't a prelude to your mother canceling Christmas. My siblings would be piled up in the back talking through their teeth at me. "Cleo what are you trying to do to us, get Christmas canceled? You big dummy! Even that three week "extra good routine" that most kids put on in the month of December wouldn't work in my mother and fathers household. They'd bring up stuff from the past and threaten to use that as motivation towards a possible Christmas cancellation. "What!" you're doing extra home work credit now? It's a little late in the game to try to bring that "B" up isn't it. Who do you think you're fooling? You kids will be out of school in a few days! Where was that extra credit work in September? Go get me a belt. Sometimes the kids had nothing to do with the cancellation of Christmas. You'd might hear, "Your father burnt the turkey", and then hear a door slam shut. It was my mother's bedroom door, and that meant my father would have to do another turkey or Christmas was canceled. Maybe some gifts that were mail ordered by my mother hadn't arrived as scheduled on Christmas Eve. She would get angry and pull Christmas right out from under us all. That's it! Game over. In most of those instances the United Parcels Service driver was just backed up, and in the morning the doorbell would ring with the gifts and Christmas was back on!

Sometimes the threat to cancel Christmas came because my mother felt she was just doing too much, and that none of the children were picking up their share of the slack. We would be called into the living room by my father, he would give us the options of a butt whooping and a cancellation of Christmas, or we could get off our young behinds and start helping our mother out a bit more. We'd all bum rush into the kitchen and ask what else we can do momma? Because for Gods sake, please don't cancel Christmas!

MOMMA DIDN'T PLAY THAT

Now my mother, aka "Annie Ruth Coney", was particularly strict when it came to her children's appearance, and behavior outside of her presence. Laws of hers and my father's were established early. My father's law was "do what your momma tells you". Here's the break down, you will always dress correctly, and this meant that a butt whooping was waiting for you if you altered any clothes after leaving home. You will behave as taught at home when away from parents; any miss behaving would result in a butt whooping. You will bathe as needed, no unpleasant body odor allowed. Unpleasant smells would be determined by the parental nose units, and handled accordingly. Teeth must be brushed a minimum of twice daily, no visible body ash, and as always you will respect other adults. Any disrespect would be given a respectful dosage of butt whooping to tighten you up. These were the guidelines that my siblings and I would follow closely, because momma didn't play that.

Now, during the winter month's temperatures would sometimes drop enough to cause a visible drying of the skin. My mother' could spot ash on a limb at two hundred yards! She'd call me over and put lotion in my hands, then tell me to hit my ashy spots. Now, the thing that made me mad was that it was this sweet smelling lotion, basically perfume. It was the stuff she wore! Nothing worse for a growing boy who still believes that girls have cooties, then to end up smelling like one! Yuck!! Can you imaging the mental stress of a young man with three older sisters, and a mother that on occasion, makes him smell like one! But you don't complain about it, because you just might open yourself up to a butt whooping. I couldn't wait to take a shower! After I would get out, I'd sneak some of my father's green after-shave. I know I used too much, because when I would walk past my father, he'd look up from his Louis Lamoure book and smile at me.

There were times when I'd come inside from playing and my father would ask me to come over to him. I'd walk over to him and he would sniff around my neck and tell my mother that the boy smells sour. Oh shoot, my playing hard outside had just elevated me to bath status! By telling my mother that I smelled sour, was my father's way of telling me that I stunk. My mother was sure to come over and sniff about my head and shoulders, and then confirm or hype up my odor to the skunk level. Yeah, and that's just what I didn't need, because perhaps the family was on it's way out shortly. Now I'd have to bathe again, and slowing the plans down could make me a target of a butt whooping. Especially if my mother had asked us kids previously not to be outside rough housing it before we head out to dinner. You'd hear her say, CLEO! I told ya'll we have to be at such n such place by such n such time! Ya'll know better than that. Now get in there and take a bath! "YES MOMMA". I'd look at my father and he'd say, "don't look at me", or "there you go". Now, at no time was I singled out; my lovely sisters also got to share in the festivities. I often enjoyed the visual sights of my mother tugging at my sister's hair, as she would readjust their braids. The tugging action as she re-braided them would cause their heads to wobble back and forth. I would try to come up with a song in my head that would have beats, matching the movements of their heads. The braiding alone was fascinating because I couldn't understand what she was really doing that gave them that clean looking final appearance. And why couldn't my sister's duplicate it? But I didn't watch too close because that might open my head up to a little combing. Did my mother go to school to learn this stuff? Or was it handed down? Oh well, who knows. Now the highlights of these hair adjustments were the conversations between my mother and my sisters. Hold still! If you hold still I'll be done quicker, or I told you this would come loose if you and Cleo didn't stop playing, or sometimes she'd say, you messed with it, and I know it. They could also possible get a smack from the comb if they talked back, so most of the time the conversations where one-sided. My parents produced American citizens with an eye for detail, respect, timeliness, couth, and cleanliness. There was no other way that my mother's kids would turn out, because my mother didn't play that.

MY BUTT LIVE THROUGH IT

From day one my parents laid down the law and the punishments for breaking the law. They never fell short of their promises as I've already outlined in the previous chapters. Some of you readers may think that my siblings and I had it hard back in the day. But I'm here to share with you that looking back on it all now; it was a very good way to keep four kids on the straight and narrow. There are many classmates that I went to school with that are currently dead or in jail. Some I've seen walking the streets on my visits to St. Petersburg Florida, where I went to high school. Some of my deceased class mates were the ones in trouble all the time, the ones in jail got involved with the wrong crowd and never got out. A parent has got to get involved with their children's lives and not leave it up to teachers, athletes, actors, and the law. My behind was in the Boy Scouts of America, The St. Petersburg Boys Choir, and my folks got involved. My father constantly told me stories of his youth, showed me how to use a fishing reel, showed me how to cook for myself, and to this day he gives me the right financial advise. (If I had only listened to the financial advice) The teachers at my schools knew my parents and were told to phone our home if I got out of hand. Now my straight "A" sisters made it hard for me though, because I followed them in high school. Sometimes the teachers would say something like;" You know your sisters never scored under a ninety Mr. Coney". Well, could you please give me some extra credit work just don't call my folks! I remember during many heated butt whoopings thinking that I was going to die if that switch-hit my legs one more time. God knows I didn't need a fresh butt whooping because I only scored an eighty-nine. Now, I've never had a beer, smoked a joint, drank a glass of wine, did any kind of drug that a doctor didn't prescribe for me, nor do I desire to in all my thirty plus years on the planet. I wonder if my folk's behavior modification methods caused me to look at the probable out comes if I took part in any of those activities. Anyhow, I utilized my interest in skateboarding to maximize my natural adrenaline rushes, so I didn't need any artificial highs. I was going to beat the odds and live through the times of hazing, peer pressure, and the rites of passage. While in a drug store one day I heard a kid tell a parent where to go. The kid could not of been more than eight or nine years old. How is this kid going to behave away from his parents if he disrespects even them? I looked at the little boy and said, don't you ever disrespect your mother! He looked at me and grabbed hold of his mother. She looked at me and said he's been that way ever since his father left, thanks for your concern sir. Wow, the importance of daddy being home with the children was never so obvious to me. I'm very lucky to have had a father that stayed home and guided me in the way I treat women. Like the many times my father told me not to hit my sister's. It was just kids playing, but in the long run it could be much more than that. I had to learn these things early, that's why he tore my butt up after Kindra and I combined to put that big knot on her head. The almighty ass whooping has been the center of much controversy these days, and paddling students at school has gone the way of the dinosaur. No one wants a stranger beating their kids, especially if the whoopings are not balanced properly in the schools. But what are you doing at home to keep your kids straight when you're not around? What do your children fear from you? My folks love kids and it shows up in the behavior of their own children. I thank GOD for allowing me to have parents strong enough to make sure my butt lived through it. Now that I'm old enough to know better, why is it that when I visit, I'm still trying to sneak a piece of my momma's sweet potato pie? Because I'm trying to eat it all before my sisters get some!

And to this day, if they get wind of it, they'll run and tell my parents, "CLEO GOT PIE"!

MY ACKNOWLEDGEMENT

GET IT OUT

My mind runneth over with colors, words, dimensions, dreams, and conscious thoughts
It spills out my mouth this over flow
Thick and gooey like a lava flow
These thoughts, passages, art, all trying to get out
I have no control over contemplations of making things float about
No control of the bright light that streams right out my eyes from my head inside
Exposing a view
A window opened, only I direct the subject matter
I'm the order that sets out of this crowed head
Containing scripts, and stories
Graphics and murals about
I want to down load this information so it can be checked out
My hands to slow
Sometimes I speak right out loud
It helps ease the mind that's pulsating to expose these feelings
These pains boiling all deep inside
From the center of my head
Languages, signs, time, flesh, spirit
All matter of things bound together in an ever-changing living putty
From my head to my hand, I write as it comes out
I write all the time, this curse, this blessing never ceases
Ideas, examples, photo shoots, concepts, new structures
Distant worlds mesh together to represent all that I make sense out of in my everyday
I see the spider
I see the grass
I feel the sun
I hear you talking, I see people walking
I notice the lint on the welcome mat

I see the gum wrapper next to the cigarette butt left of the bum
I realize I think too much, this I can't help
But I put it down; I write it to let some pressure out
The texture of your hair interest me
That old building interest me
What year is that penny on the ground?
That road is smooth and black
That one is gray and rough
That little girl has two Afro puffs
Rockem-Sockem Robots, old furniture musk
Ultra contemporary homes, and purple gremlin emblems on my mind with other stuff
Like fresh seafood, and a scab over a wound
Is my insurance up to date? And watch that plane go zoom
Old episodes of Manix and Room Two Twenty Two
After school Spam sandwiches
Continental drift and spoiled milk
Air traffic, land traffic, commercial traffic, or is there a Rooms To Go
Sexy dancers, new car smells, a kids face in the window
Plumbing that leaks and is a ditch also a creek?
My mind rambles daily, questions upon questions
There is no end
Nothing passes my mind without getting in
If I see it, it gets contemplated
Yes, it's a strain, but it's all I've known since the time I was three
So much going on inside
Information without foundation
My mind is working over time
The symptoms I have I know not what to call
I'll I want is to share it all

TABLE OF CONTENTS

MY ACKNOWLEDGEMENT: *GET IT OUT* lxix

1) OUT HERE 1
2) A LITTLE MO' FASTER 2
3) BLIND MICE 3
4) THE FORGOTTEN 4
5) BOUND GAGGED TIED & BURNED 5
6) BERGAMOT DAYS 6
7) CATCH TWENTY TWO 7
8) CLEAN SLATES 8
9) YELLOW 9
10) GREEN 10
11) HAND OUT 11
12) HOLLA 12
13) HOLOGRAPHIC TELEVISION 13
14) HONEY 14
15) IN A SECOND 15
16) LIFE DANCES WITH DEATH 16
17) LOUD 18
18) DAMN! 19
19) PARDON MY SUFFERING 20
20) SHAQ DREAMS 21
21) SKATE SPIRIT 23
22) MANS MISTAKES 24
23) LIFE'S TALE 25
24) OVER THE TOP 26
25) MIND OVER MATTER 28
26) MY LIFE'S CAVITY 30
27) THE OUTSIDE INFLUENCE 31
28) PENNY GARDEN 32
29) SO I LEFT 33
30) THANG 34
31) THE BUS 35
32) THE COLLECTION 36
33) THE LIE 37
34) THE NATURAL 38

lxxi

35) THE DANCER 39
36) THE VOID 40
37) THE WORLD EATS 41
38) THE WRATH OF CHARLIE 43
39) TO MY SISTERS 44
40) MISFOCUS OF EARTHS PEOPLE 45
41) GOLDEN PLANTERS 46
42) LET LIGHT IN 47
43) I'M ON THE OUTSIDE LOOKING OUT 48
44) BLONDE 49
45) BULLETS RUN FAST 50
46) BOBBING BAGS 51
47) THE ALTERNATIVE 52
48) AND I SAW HER LAY 53
49) EYES OPENED 55
50) IN THE PRESENCE 56
51) A CHANGE 57
52) THANKS 58
53) THE DOLLS 59
54) THE AIR 60
55) PATH 61
56) CONSPICUOUS CONSUMPTION 64
57) NEW CHERRY BLOSSOM DEW 66
58) THE WORLD GOES CRUNCH 67
59) THE EXOTIC 69
60) GENIE 70
61) THE GOOD OLE' DAYS 71

OUT HERE

out here underneath this heavy blue canopy
dotted with puffy clouds
rusted tin roofs are a reminder of those hot lemonade days
a place where everyone worked at the mines
a place where home was just down the street from those huge white hills of powdered dinosaur bones
rocking chairs on porches, clothes lines separating backyards, no no grocer nearby
but someone is selling something to eat, greens, fish sandwiches, a a chicken or two
oh, and the church is full on Sundays
across the way there is openness for as far as the eye can see
little brush trees highlight the landscape
oh, and the children play through the yards
a short car ride in any direction will bring you to a rusted nonworking piece of machinery, once brand new
tractors, trailers, pumps, buses, and all sorts of automobiles litter little the surrounding plain
the earth has claimed forty five percent of these old man made devices, which still have strength in their uselessness
why don't these tired souls move on?
why do they stay out here underneath this vastness?
even the nearest town is dated and far away
well, we are not to question these people who's hard work has passed through generations
what's this?...generations?
that may be the key, perhaps there is joy in repetition.
this place is full of stories that must be written
this old, empty, isolated and small town sits, and waits,...
for something.

CLEO C. CONEY JR.

A LITTLE MO' FASTER

Faced with a problem
Undying needs
She started out young
Only seventeen
Big cities, big lights
Big plans to unfold
LA, Miami, New York
Knocking on every door
Focused on her dreams
No resume' in hands
What's that spinning?
Oh, a ceiling fan
A little mo' faster
In every state a house
In every house a couch
Late night casting
She just wants to be a star
She knows every nobody
And everybody who knows someone
Nobody knows her she's just for fun
A little mo' faster
Inside her mind
The old dreams still alive
Television, video's, movies
All the media glory
But behind closed doors
The same ole story
A little mo' faster
A vicious cycle
Broken promises and dreams
Another Cinderella under a fella
Still wearing his blue jeans
Unglued legs serve as a deposit
For those young angels with out wings
A little mo' faster

BLIND MICE

Pasteurized ideas funneled through the farms of sameness
Delivered highly packaged, highly touted
Shined and stamped as the newest, the next, the best
Organized by those who love Elvis, but hate Marvin Gaye
And wearing the repeated, the played again
Clothing of lifelessness
These are the days of variation on recycle
Sell the old as the new and do it quickly
Electronic messages piped into the homes and automobiles of the public
Geared to increase purchases, create images of greatness
Hide the real truth's about who's selling what, and where the product is actually coming from
Perceived or otherwise, when what we need is physical exercise
Loose some couched calories, take a deep breath
Step back and then pick up a book

THE FORGOTTEN

I am that piece of lint on the floor of the washhouse
Filled with mites and old chips from card board boxes
Hardened, lonely, not even cleaned up
Because behind the clothes dryer of life I am the forgotten
One day I will be found and swept away
There is no use for lint, so I am useless
A purple, beige, and pink clump
rarely visited by a roach or cricket
Because of the heat of life's dryer
I have seen the sun of love only once, as I fell out of the clothesbasket to the floor
It was bright, warm, and caring
All that doesn't matter now; for dust is my reality, lint is my name
Remember me before I fell, a bit of everything
from a shirt to a pair of pants
I moved about, but now, now I'm still
Remember me my love
I will never forget you

BOUND GAGGED TIED & BURNED

Sluggishly I step knee deep
in this thick and gooey land of creditors
All the while they pull at my very being
Like cords of rubber fashioned to twenty pound bricks and tied to each of my bodies joints
From my fingers to my ankles taxes pour over my body in the consistency of tar, but hotter than lava
Only the two straws coming out of my nose allowing me to breathe and the whites of my eyes can be seen
My hair is a mass of tangled insects called work related issues
Heaps of these bugs crawl upon my head and back, tiring my neck from their constant shivering
Threats from my landlord evaporate the water from my mouth, and stomach
Oh, how I thirst
The disappointment I fear to give to my parents weighs upon my spirit like two refrigerators on my back
No one is able to count the number of times the whips of panic have sliced into my flesh
My mind is afflicted with bruises brought on by the lack of sleep
There is no sleep
Only the evil known as cash money, will lift these burdens brought on by society, and the needs of men in my time
The planet will survive
In my time on this planet, men will die and be born
Will they be free, or amongst the walking dead?
That, is now the question

CLEO C. CONEY JR.

BERGAMOT DAYS

Clankity clank these tubes travel
Off and on, light teases my vision through glass windows
Quiet comes and goes as it pleases
Moving from chair to chair, interrupting conversation
Eyes move across clothing, bodies, and faces
Sometimes eyes catch and cause blinking
Sometimes eyes catch and create smiles
Someone is on the train going nowhere
Many are on the way to jobs and homes
Most are alone
Women dominate this place old and young
But all in various shades of brown and black
Looking up at the nearest woman
Her gaze is studied as it covers another
I look left quickly and a smile is created
I look right quickly and a head is made to turn
I'm very comfortable now as the smell of freshly styled black hair
enters my nares
Causing emotions and memories to be stirred
I remember back as I smile to myself
To the days when I first encountered those smells
Hot combs & hair grease
I sit as the tube becomes black briefly
as a tunnel is passed through
How wonderful each of these individual black women are
I am wrapped in the bosom of black grace
Taken back to my mothers place in my mind
While my sisters heads she styled and primped
I find comfort in this moment of warmth
I'm what you call pleased to be black

Catch Twenty Two

Circumstances, life's envelope,
A current situation including a present thought
A financial obligation to start you sweating
This girl is that girl, and I've been there as well
An objection to my minds erection for things nice
Puts me into a jar of confusion lid tight
So I'm rocking the jar
Trying to break free of the bed I've made
Of the present path I'm traveling
I long for a constant smile and a sweet wife to build on
But a gravel filled throat, prevents me to have spoken to the one
Who could be the one
So out here in the rain I remain
Hardened and sad

CLEAN SLATES

I'm watching these babies with smiles on their faces
Bouncing on laps
Little heads moving back
I'm thinking how nice to see those innocent eyes
Little minds all open wide
Only wanting to eat
Stay warm
Take a nap
Mouths drooling
No shame
They don't know that
Existing in a bliss
That's blind to the kind at home that loves them back
They're little clean slates
But through example
Assimilation of their minds
These young toddlers learn to mind their folk's habits and prejudice's
Isn't it a shame?
How we negate a blissful state
Just by writing in the minds
Of those little clean slates

YELLOW

Yellow silky smooth Carmel colored beauty
My eyes have seen the silhouette many times
Always a group of unauthorized butterflies would make me weak
Taking the man out of my knees
Yellow silky smooth Carmel colored beauty
My neck straining to position my nares in the vicinity of your sweet smelling perfume
That only you in combination makes sweeter
Yellow silky smooth Carmel colored beauty
Did I dare risk a "no" seeking a yes?
She must be taken, it has to be, no princess this fine
could possible be free
Yellow silky smooth Carmel colored beauty
Many a time I've run over to your person and stated my plea
Only deep inside my own head did our conversation exist
Yellow silky smooth Carmel colored beauty
You wrestle away my cool with just a glance
You tie my chest in knots and my car won't start
Like an alien abduction I'm floating about
With you on my mind I might pass out
Yellow silky smooth Carmel colored beauty
I'm caught in your mist, your strong gravity promising bliss
And it's very inconvient to be in, but I don't want to get out of
Yellow silky smooth Carmel colored beauty
After seeing you on Friday I've made it my duty
To get to know you real well, and treat you like my lady

CLEO C. CONEY JR.

GREEN

I feel green
Not like a rookie
But like a new leaf
I feel green today
Fresh, a new, rapidly expanding
Boy, do I feel green
Like new hundred dollar bills
Crisp and ready
I feel green, a glow
About to take hold
I feel green
And I can't wait to show
This feeling I have
Bright, clean, and fresh
I feel green today
And I want everybody to know
This feeling of green
Green, green, green!
Looking up at the blue sky
I feel green today

HAND OUT

Can you help an old man out?
I will work for food, but prefer a cash handout
I need two quarters to make my cab fare
I'm a disabled VET
Homeless who's bled for our country
Now on the streets I live
Give me a mothefunkin dime!
Brother, help another brother out
Can I interest you in a bean pie?
To help chase white demons out
I'm with the fire department collecting
I'm feeding the kids
Were collecting for our church
Please help us and give
My family and me just got evicted
I lost my job after thirty years
Help me I'm blind, buy my pencils for a dime
Jehovah will save you just give us two dollars
I'm selling chocolate for my school
And I have cookies from the girl scouts
We're only in the neighborhood today
With our stereo close outs
Help, give, buy
Break me a piece of your money off
I don't care how much you're paid
Because I have fresh flowers, hot peanuts
And ice cold lemonade
I am in your pockets, much worse in your head
I'll bring guilt, pain, disbelief, and sorrow to your day
I'm the open hand on the corner that gets shaked seldom
Sometimes I'm in your way
I'm your neighbor help me in my yard
I am your child with needs, with a passed down disease
I am your spouse, I am your parent, I am your friend
I'm also on the Internet
I am your sibling, and I am on the corner with my hand out

HOLLA

At what time did I hear the shout?
At no time
No, it wasn't a scream
Nah sir,
I'll tell you what I heard
I heard a man holla
I heard the end of him
I heard a man holla
Him, he witnessed death coming
No shout, not a scream
I heard him holla
Cause death was all about
I knew this man
He wasn't the type to shout for help
He wasn't the type who'd scream if frightened
This man now dead, holla'd
Cause his life had come to an end

HOLOGRAPHIC TELEVISION

Tongue sliding, side walking replication of your early vision
You ain't no mistake
Your fault is correct in its deep, deep, state of melted ways
Press on my minds pink
Creep through walls of altering dreams
Dear to me to be dearly departed
You ain't nothing but a holographic television
Egos ago I was inside my own head, but days ago inside your bed
Wrapped up in a false sense of security
Letting your outside inside my deep side
The end not far behind, your beam directly in my eyes
You ain't nothing but a holographic television
The all of me in the part of you
Smiling at me although I saw right through
No shield can hide the wrong you do
You ain't nothing but a holographic television
I need a change

HONEY

A warm memory rinsed in puppy love replays in my mind including the smells
All it took was a soft sax song played today from long ago to trigger a grin upon my face
Eyes sparkle with the sights stored away
As swiftly as she entered a chapter of my life
Time turns pages faster away
The feeling is happy when these moments are replayed
I know each time the song is played
again shall I remember her story
Again smells will fill my head
Her video remains unedited, stored deep in my mind
Waiting for the key that is a song
To release warm memories rinsed in puppy love

IN A SECOND

a favorite painted picture
a look through a window
a photograph of times past
a image in the mind
a meaning only you enjoy fully
a moment of good feelings
a warm glow inside
a smile showing on the outside
a gleam in the eye
a second has gone by
all at once

CLEO C. CONEY JR.

LIFE DANCES WITH DEATH

Life dances with death on a daily basis
Life dances with death so don't you test it
For sure if not now then later
You'll get your turn on this I'll bet you
It is the nature of life to dance with death
One inch closer and it will claim you
An hour earlier it could have been you
You missed that flight for a reason
In your mind death wasn't an issue
Until after the news
You can count on it like the morning
It only visits once in a lifetime
This much is true
Near death experiences don't count
Cause death didn't claim you
Clinically dead is debatable but…
I guess death really didn't have you
We all live and part of life is the death preview
Glimpses of other deaths before your turn confronts you
You can take comfort in knowing, that everyone who has lived
Has passed through
That part of life we don't look forward too
No one wants to be in line, or on death row but…
Eventually this fact hits you
Friends and family have already gone on back to the earth
As we all do
We learn lessons
Pass them down
So each generation can learn from the mistakes we made during our time
So short, so sweet
You won't get a round two
No extra lives like video games do
No extra time on earth after death claims you
From the womb to the tomb
For the time between is up to you to decide your life's direction

Build up, or tear down
What are you going to do while you're around?
Life dances with death on a daily basis
One stray bullet and you'll change places
On earth to a part of the earth
Is it your time or a timely mistake?
That lowers you down six feet into the grave
Live life to its fullest
Don't wait for the perfect time
Cause death has its own schedule
But death is always on time

CLEO C. CONEY JR.

LOUD

Green and great they were
Bold and in bloom they stood
But their beauty wasn't loud enough
Hills rolled across the vastness of my gaze
Mountains rose up above me in their greatness
Still this country wasn't loud enough
Nor was it liquid enough for me
I longed for the sound of the tide crashing on the shore
I yearned for summer storms thunder roars
The smell of salt air could quench my longing for home
This rich red clay soil cannot hold my feet
The sands of the beach they seek
My figure beneath the shadow of palms swaying in the breeze
Memories take me away from these old pines
Flash backs remove me from those little creeks and rivers flow
The depths of the gulf they do not know
The bounty of a days saltwater fish catch,
these hills cannot produce
The calls of the hawks have not the strength
to erase the laughter of the gulls
Evening sounds of the woods should not try to compete with the
calmness of a beaches evening sundown
How great a place this earth is, so much beauty there is
My heart stays near the bays
My mind remembers those salad days
This beautiful Georgia place is just not loud enough for me

DAMN!

Her frame as perfect as a flawless diamond
She moves through the room like melted butter
Softly, and with a cat like smoothness
Each word that leaves her sweet fruits split to form lips
As deliberate and as sure as its delivery
The proud neck she possesses gently positions her ever-soft face, in my longing direction
Dinner seems incidental and like that of a prop
My shyness hidden in the excitement of her warm presence
I'm moved by even her shadow
How long can a man hold his heart?
How long can he suppress the issue in his head?
Overwhelmed by his own indecision
Brought on by the infection of her beauty
This he cannot deny
There is much to be said, and much time that must go by
Before it can be said
So as not to frighten away the very thing that he has run from for years
He has realized that in her company nothing else matters
So her company is all that he desires
So it begins

PARDON MY SUFFERING

Pardon my suffering
I didn't mean to get in your way
I know your life is busy, and I shouldn't have slept in your doorway
Pardon my suffering
I surely didn't mean to bring unpleasantness to your day
With all the things that you must do
I know there was no time to be stalled
The dime I asked for was way too much I'm sure
Pardon my suffering
Please excuse my appearance
I know I'm dirty, and smelly
You see in no home do I dwell
Pardon my suffering
Yes I know it's a hassle to donate a half a sandwich
Anyway, I know of a great trash bin with food within
Pardon my suffering please sir
I shouldn't have looked at your date
Pardon my suffering
I hear your every word
Yes, a job would be nice!
But no one will hire me in this state of poor health and homelessness
Only one set of clothes do I own
Please pardon my suffering
My condition I did not wish, and do not wish upon thee
So please during your hectic day, and busy nights
Or while you're resting at home in the warmth of your surroundings
Please, pardon my suffering

SHAQ DREAMS

A congregation of ladies, of and every variation
Do their best in a subtle demonstration
To stride as close as they can
Hoping to be embraced in their very own Shaq dreams
I'm talking about those females who gather
partly clothed no matter
Doing what they hope will end their dilemmas
of no financial status
I mean their looking for a fellow who's doing well
Oh yeah, gold digging and sweating means
Suckers for dough only none they've grown
Double fronting freaks, it's not a nice thing
Although healthy and fine, loaded with candy coated lips aloof
Swaying hips to boot, using all their youth as bait,
to end the lifestyle they hate
Lack of cash so they stash a hope for Shaq dreams
Living in the A-T-L it's easy to see this well
As honey laden Georgia peaches turn into leeches when a successful man's cash can be seen
They may say no, or they're minding their own
But the truth is in their actions
As semi celebrity, after semi celebrity they drool,
most ending up on stools used like tools
Never gaining so called dues, and seeing their Shaq dreams
They gather in clubs packed, stacked, looks nonlacked
The plan is easy; find a man to please thee
Here he comes, look at them check their buns, I hope he sees me
Now let me be fair to the ladies with their own means
Creating a route to see dreams
Non-assisted by an athlete who's gifted, or an actor in blue jeans
They are the backbone not caught on the phone
talking about whom they've seen
The unrealistic ladies soon to become statistics of one-night stands
Never ever gaining the man that makes up their Shaq dreams
Breath of the year, passion of longing dears
Caught up in a hopeless battle, percentages against their mettle

CLEO C. CONEY JR.

To withstand the pressure they create upon themselves to nicely borrow upon someone else's wealth
Particularly those well paid for not saving one life
These girls depend on their Shaq dreams

SKATE SPIRIT

gray-white concrete rushes by me
smoothly I glide, while these legs flex
a wide smile interrupts staid cheeks
air fills these lungs, as I stay young,
while my heart beats
one with the board beneath my feet
angles I seek, speed answers my wheels
trees and sky merge forming a welcome blur
now I am free

MANS MISTAKES

I killed an ice cube today
I took it out of the freezer
I laid it on some hot concrete, and then I pulled up a seat
I killed an ice cube today cause I had nothing else to do
I watched as it reacted to its new surroundings,
by slowly melting away
I killed an ice cube today
Out in the drive way
I watched it slowly sweat
I watched water roll away
What was once a firm block of ice minding it's own,
seem to slowly change shape
It lost its form
I, me, did this deed to innocent ice
No threat to anyone
No need for me to treat it this way
But no
I reached in and grabbed one out of it's home the freezer
Just to have my way
This individual block, a cube to some in this form
Lost everything that it was, when it melted out on the hot driveway
Directly under the sun
I killed an ice cube today for no reason at all
The ice that was a cube, then a puddle, evaporated into the air
The cube of ice from the freezer I did take for my eyes
Is no longer there

Life's Tale

Misty, drizzly, and nameless, I left this quiet place
I had to push on through this ever-winding passage
Rough and filled with texture these aged oak trees
Never complained about the running squirrels in their branches
Shaded from the hot star that shone brightly, I rested until the calls
Of the night animals insisted that I become a part of their song
Bones aged but hardened as time was taken to stop a moment and
Contemplate just how far I've come
A deep breathe as I pondered my next move
A smile for GOD because in my life's strife
There was good in it all

CLEO C. CONEY JR.

OVER THE TOP

I'm presently all glittery inside
This silly childish butterfly feeling in my chest
Has my spirit all a glow
I know the reason
I met the reason twice
Most recently at a football gathering over some friends
Petite and pretty
Full of fun
This golden black woman has my mind on the run
Thousands of contemplations
While I try to watch these NFL playoffs
Countless possibilities of will she, or will she not
Give me the time it will take
For this man to generate
A union of souls
Ok, ok, I know I've got to slow down
But it's her smell, her alluring glare
Her full and healthy butt
Held up so sweet and nice
This brother looked twice!
Shameless am I in the lust of her physical being
Longing am I in the need of this woman walking by my side
Hand in hand we will stroll through this changing life
Younger this day, older this night
Safe in her arms my heart and mind will be
Less stressful day to day it will be
Emotional bliss would satisfy me
Oh, how I would work to please
This petite package with the golden feet
That look like candy to me, mmmmmmmmm!
I can taste my life for the better with her in place
oooohhhh! I can sleep better with her in my place
What of this wonderment and do I dare share
The powerful feelings bursting from within this man
I've looked upon the images in my minds warehouse
That special place where things of magnitude stand out

AMBIENT ECHOES

I can't erase, I make haste, rushing back to those beautiful images
And I know how dangerous the beautiful ones are
They will lift you up enough to let you down
But I must chance my hearts injury
I must chance my minds peace
To get upon the one I've wanted most in years
And build more than a house
Head forward into this wind of a woman's soul
As it blows me away across the plain of all that is sure
I drift longingly into a realm I'm not familiar with
A place of risk and great pain
And yet here I am smiling as it happens
What is this thing that has me held fast?
I will not argue, but I will ask the question of this woman
Only time will tell of the outcome
But for now I only seek the shelter of her glow and the warmth of her lips on mine
She is the dear that I have longed for
It is clear to me now; she is the sweet Promised Land
From which my life and soul will grow

CLEO C. CONEY JR.

MIND OVER MATTER

Yeah, I can rock it with the best of the said best
Lyrical attack force plus one, me one
The one to look out for as I climb up life's ladder
An example that makes others sadder
Because my focus is sure
Keep your head up as I reach for the stars
The job I have I created from inside my head
The passion I have is from the heart
The passion I treasure is writing the say
Oh, I'm with the time
I've flexed, I've become more complex
As the delivery of the rhetoric grows
I'm just getting started
Check your ears as I flow on into your mind
Like smoke in lungs
No chance for failure, I can't let nothing derail
Ah,
The man chosen to create pieces of dreams
And pour them into written containers to share with ya
Solid in my tongue, putting pressure on the softly spoken
So they might hardened up with the spirit as the one
Me one, has done
And will continue like the heavens above
Even after I'm dust, part of the earth's crust
Pulled up into form, flesh because water was added with GOD'S breath
And now I exist to exert thought before my exit from this place
My mind is the clay that forms words of fired ceramic for others to contemplate
Leave the televisions, pull up some grass, and sit on dat azz
Listen to the world with your eyes closed
The beginning of the method to learn
This is the lesson, day one
Now open your eyes and combine the sight, it's all clearer now
Yet shall my words be repeated in question
A study of all things lovely

No limits set, no goal to far
The hands instructed by the mind
The spirit is in thy hands
The ink flows to inscribe the words and the wonders of the universe placed
The order of which cannot be planned
It is of it's self divine
So listen to this man now in the flesh of the earth mixed with water and GOD'S breath
Molten man is the blood that flows
I just keep shaking those who would try to undo my health
My rise in wealth
Like a puppy shakes a chew toy
Keeping them guessing
I'm electing to continue my verbal barrage
An alphabet medley constructed for pleasure, with meanings to study
Words for the masses
Corrected sight for those with mind glasses
I'm on a new mission to produce
No I'm not wishing for a name for my blessings
Psychic shuffling
Tempered never idle
Pause and you'll miss all I've left for your ears to deliver to your mind
Your life I assist

CLEO C. CONEY JR.

MY LIFE'S CAVITY

She was my life's cavity I knew I had to pull her out
She was the truest form of sweetness,
this dilemma made me shout
Inspired by her beauty my mouth watered at her view
I would contemplate her calves as they flexed
While she strolled about the house
She was the most concentrated lust-creating figure
I've ever sampled
No fire department had the skills to douse
The flames she created in my loins
no other woman can do this now
No relationship can last because of lust, hot sex and great views
Something more has to come about
A meeting of the minds will deliver
a longer lasting union between figures
But as a man I had to find that out
So I took a chance, let my mind follow my pants
The answer was already known
This woman would not deliver
more than the pain of a superbly built figure
Can't help but will to happen, rubber necking,
other men's necks snapping
Offering up to the mind small in nature
Dependant on what her figure could deliver,
not just from the chosen
But to become one of her many selections
This I could not stand
So apart we are, apart we shall stay
And through these years that have past
her frame I still contemplate
But my life is much better now with out the cavity aggravate
Of her sweet, sweet, everything, that caused this figure so much pain

THE OUTSIDE INFLUENCE

In the beginning it was out parents
Later on it was our teachers
Sometime in life it will be our mates
For some of us it will be our religion
Our friends will be it as well
It's also the food we eat
But for the longest time
Since man has walked
It has mostly been the gravity at our feet

PENNY GARDEN

In a penny garden it's easy for two old wooden clothespins to become two toy automobiles
In a penny garden empty matchboxes become toy blocks
In a penny garden two girls use a water hose screwed to the tap as a jump rope
In a penny garden old grandma buttons become checkerboard pieces
In a penny garden a sock around a folded hanger becomes a perfect doll tent
In a penny garden no sugar is in the Kool-Aid
In a penny garden ice cold water is called city punch
In a penny garden an old Philco television with one channel reception is what's on the tube
In a penny garden neighbors visit because there are no phones
In a penny garden air conditioning is an open window provided there's a breeze
In a penny garden everything is used twice after it's thrown away
In a penny garden there is much love, much pain
In a penny garden life is always better one cent away

SO I LEFT

Paper or plastic is all they ask you
How yah doing not coming through'em
So I left
With my list crossed out, I load the cabinets
Phone rings, it's the girl
So I left
Cruised real slowly in traffic, plenty of time to go
Cop says no pull over
Red and blue flashing
Did I do something wrong?
Oh, I'm free to go
So I left
Now I'm late for my date
Lady's no lady
Mouth flapping wide, no excuses, and no lies
The noise increases, only she knows why
So I left
Busted a move over to my homies
Cold chilling to three am
Next stop the apartment for sleep
Got a bed to get in
So I left

CLEO C. CONEY JR.

THANG

This thang has got me tripping
I mean, this smooth silky black something
Shoot, I should be silent, but nah, nah
There's a tongue that can't be tied
A thirst for dark sweet maple syrup walking up right
Right, yeah, oh so right,
Thick and juicy near the thighs
An hour glass that makes all men suffer
And that onion bringing tears to my eyes
This thang has got me tripping
A bright white smile has got me thinking and re-thinking
Man you should just slow down it's out of bounds
So I sit on my hands, I sit on my tongue
Shouldn't I release, will I be sprung?
Ok, ok, take a deep breath and now breathe,
aaaaahhhhhh!
Whew she's up in my mind like fresh sweet potato pie
And everyday is a holiday when she passes by
This thang has got me tripping
This smooth silky black something
Do ya'll understand me?
Do ya'll comprehend this lump in my chest that's thumping?
Over and over again I see us humping and I can't make it stop
Cause this thang is hot and smooth
This thang is true, and in my mind she's cut a groove
To let me know her thang, is really something

THE BUS

I don't want to ride the bus
I don't want to sit next to, whom?
I don't like traveling slow
I don't like frequent stops
Please, I don't want to ride the bus
I don't want to ask him or her to please move over
I don't want to share my seat at this time
No, I won't move on over
I don't want to search for change
And have to look at the forty five percent of the riders that look dazed
I'm not interested in the gum in the seats, loud children
Or the half eaten sandwich next to my foot
I don't want to ride the bus
I don't want to stand next to the curb
I don't mind old folks, but I don't want to talk about Willie Mays
I don't know what transfer you should take, lady I don't care
I don't know when this big gas guzzling contraptions gonna stop
I just know my way
I don't want to ride the bus
I don't enjoy small talk
I don't know why these drivers get fat
I don't know how much they're paid
I don't enjoy other people's conversations
I don't want to get in it
I don't want to ride the bus
School, City, or National
I don't know who invented these big boxes
But I've got to ride them until the day I'm paid

CLEO C. CONEY JR.

THE COLLECTION

The collection as it is called is much more than that
these ridgit cuddly dozens of bears stand guard
at my sister's house
rows of fuzzy stoned eyes always looking in my direction
As I pass them during my visit's
they, the dozens, call out to my sister in the night
while she's fast asleep
Buy another! they so often tell her
Increase our ranks amongst your home
We, who supply thee with fur therapy, are motionless until picked
up and squeezed
Our ranks must grow, so we shall not be forgotten
They cry out with their telepathy
The strength of their influence is seen in the delivery of another
bear by those from outside of Andrea's home
So now and from now on, the bear's ranks grow
small and tiny, large with fur briny
there they stand, lean, and lay
until their picked up to be squeezed and looked upon
But do not, I say please sir, do not pass the purple one my way
He is the one I fear most, as many a time I've found him next to
me when I wake
I know it is Andrea who places him there, but I believe it's the
bear having his way

THE LIE

A breeze, too cool for summer, passed through a field teaming with ancient wrinkled oak trees
The oaks had become the unwilling participants in the removal of life from the victims stolen in the night because of a lie
This breeze moved through the field of oaks kissing each body enough to cause a swinging motion like a pendulum, which aggravated the flies
Death had been slow for some, but sure
No one knows their names, except for the charred bodies that lay on the ground down the road a piece
Here, in a pool of calm, only the black square and rectangle outlines made of ash, leave any clue that a home once stood here
Inside the lines crispy bodies lie twisted and cooked to the bone
All women and children, some with single bullet holes through their skulls
Others missing chunks of skull which were removed by the various axes of the murderers
Just across the way, a stream fed by a spring hurries over smooth stones along its daily trip
Today, the stream makes its trip beneath a sky so blue only the rays of the sun interrupt its majesty
Birds and cloud's still bothered by the death in the night do not wish to pass over the scene far below
So, for as far as the eye can see, only blue is seen.
Here in these parts the bible is the anchor of all who live in fear of GOD, yet do ungodly acts in the name of the Lord
It seems some where along the way, GOD created a different heaven, with a different set of commandments
There is no more singing in the little town that was, just the sound of leaves and bodies swaying and rustling in the wind
The seeds planted in the spring will grow tall and bear fruit
The planters will not enjoy the fruit of their labor this year, or the next year, or the year after
There will be no one else to point the finger at next time, no one to lie on
Just a mirror to look in and ask, why?

CLEO C. CONEY JR.

THE NATURAL

the smile is what gets me,
the walk makes me focus,
she's so fine
I think I'll just toast my orange juice to those great looks
crack a grin to myself, and say, "perfect" to those buns on her bod
so smooth and taught
a brother doesn't question the in plain daylight visual onslaught
it's taken in stride as she glides on by
none of her beauty is store bought

THE DANCER

The two biggest candy apples
I've ever witnessed
Sugar coated chocolate drops
Or you could say raspberry applicious
There they hung
Rounded and full of nectar
I wanted to bite them
But nah, it was way to soon
To even go there
They were two-toned honeycombs
Frequently wetted
By the bubble gum colored muscle
Known as her tongue
I eliminated all of my surroundings
Except for this gorgeous set of lips
They were the kind you write home about
The kind that deserved tips
This woman's lips that caught my eye
Belonged too no ordinary gal
She was from way out west
I believe she said Cal
Not my normal modus operandi
She could be considered not my type
But that smooth brown skin
In combination with those over sized lips
Was enough to make this brother
Change his mind

THE VOID

Like a wooden duck in a pond
Set up to attract the real billed
I'm stumbling through my life like I'm in the way
This is supposed to be my script
I'm supposed to be the star of my life story
But I feel like an extra
I feel like the only empty room in a Twenty Room house
I'm frozen with out ice
Motionless in my own wake
A pen with out ink
How will I get out of this strange funk?
What will undo this feeling of no love?
A better way of believing is to shake this unveiling
An umbilical rope made of steel
Suspending my soul in this void
Some how should just be lifted out, or pulled up
If I could just feel the sun on my brow I know I'd be let out
Until this blessing is reached, here shall I roam
Alone in my life
With out myself
Dwelling in a void

AMBIENT ECHOES

THE WORLD EATS

A salt and pepper fry consisting of squid parts
A smoked section of turkey necks stewed up in navy beans
Mashed plantains cooked while still green
Others enjoying the broiled skin of a salmon
A pigs hips roasted slowly and served with rice
Choice cuts of raw tuna are preferable to cuts of potatoes French-fried
Big hunks of beef called steaks
Ground up beef served with a box of helper and collected meal worms heated slowly
Turtle sections basted with a broth of veggies
Young lambs kept from the sun and milk fed before dead
Please many from the English run
Chickens served in hundred of ways
Crickets gathered, legs and heads removed before cooking
And hot dogs in buns, mustards the normal do
Dogs that catch Frisbees could end up in dinner trays
Fins of sharks used in soups
The blood of oxen mixed and served with milk
A variety of larvae are popped down quickly, and some chewed to enjoy the goo
Goats roasted on an open fire, a wild cat has been known to be eaten too
Rabbits, monkeys, opossums, raccoons, rats and large American iguanas
Have been put in a pot as well, well done and done well
Fly babies consumed for the protein
Snakes and spiders didn't fare as well
Various vegetables well known and plants with thorns less gorged on
Dolphins, blue jays, and all sorts of creature's eggs
Gobbled down putting smiles on once stomachs empty faces
On the darker side, men have eaten men and would have continued
If man had tasted as good as horse meat, dried jellyfish, polar bear, or a whales stomach contents

CLEO C. CONEY JR.

    We eat what we eat
    Where we live is what we see
    Sometimes because of tradition, sometimes because it's free
    Make no mistake about it
    Don't get grossed out
    You could just as well of been eating squirrels instead of Mickey D's...or both

THE WRATH OF CHARLIE

you could never figure if this dusty old mutt's bark was bigger than his bite
charlie he was called, charlie called he never came
charlie never looked at you unless you couldn't see him
stayed outside in the sun and rain
threaten he would with his growls, whiskers gnarled, hair on his back stood
he allowed us to ride on the skateboard ramp next to the holes he dug
charlie, this old dusty, rusty mutt some would say no good
kept all the thugs away, where we played and lived in the hood

CLEO C. CONEY JR.

TO MY SISTERS

I cracked on your ashy knees
Busted on your bellbottom jeans
I talked about your Afro puffs
I even said you drank warm milk of fluffs!
But you know I still love you
I went off on your butter teeth
Cracked a smile when you slipped off your feet
Poked fun at the knot on your head
Told daddy you did it instead
But you know I still love you
Now I'll still show your old pictures
And point out your lips whiskers
Make light of the crust in your eyes
And run from your morning sigh
But you know I still love you

MISFOCUS OF EARTHS PEOPLE

You say it's sparkling sand no longer than slivers of glass
Hills and hills of ground down powder
Heated earth turned white after birth
A light seen from space, another test during the race
To see what group of men could empty the most sons of men
And remove their individual spirits
Ah yes, mounds and mounds serve as our reminder
Of what great minds can produce to pull us all under
But a big rock hurling through space could spell doom, and the end of this place
Very interesting you might say, that we worry about men across the seas
And build war-machines that can kill from hundreds of miles away
It's just plain stupid
Why kill each other when each other are all we have?
Earth is the roof over our heads
Better plan and put minds together
Maybe we can save our only home
From a big chunk of ice and gravel

CLEO C. CONEY JR.

GOLDEN PLANTERS

I tippy toe around her golden planters
Beneath her ankles begins my attachment
Smooth and evenly spread, the color captures me
Yellow graham cracker gravy covers them,
Yet cannot hide these perfect slipper molds
They are like jewels to be shown through glass cases
They draw me to their side without my permission
I look upon them in awe, these golden planters without ridge,
Without scale, decorated on the tips with rich color
Balanced, sleek like jungle cats, but no threat shall these kittens make
They are of themselves, separate and bold, they exude sexiness and cleanliness
They are the fixation, which turns into flirtation, ye golden planters
Part of the total package, these planters of gold
The icing on the cake, the prize in my candy, the focus of my eyes
Lovely, golden planters

AMBIENT ECHOES

Let light In

A concentrated effort to raise up from the dust
No bootstraps, no free rides,
No older relative in the upper crust to help these brothers out
They come into the world with chains on, and then they are lowered into the ground with ropes
My soul is hurting but I won't give up hope
My mind is churning options and the possibilities of escape
While the nation is coming up with more ways to hold my race down and back
Cause the world is changing slowly from white to black
They can't stand that so we've got to get inside our roots
Got to relate to our ancestors past
Like the Olmecs, great builders in the golden age these brothers were way advanced
We've got to get inside our roots; we've got to study ancestors long gone
Before the great Pharaohs brothers sang the whole earths song
Tossing and turning each night it's hard to sleep
Every day I'm seeing brothers and their families out on the streets
Young and black with great potential, why are they blowing off the essentials
Like arithmetic, and the sciences, for new cars and appliances
No longer focused on the future and the past, but only seeing the present
Our downfall will be the lesson cause the present is ruled by the past, and the future looks unpleasant
Cause these young video watchers are stuck on the present
Forget about all those Benz dreams and big crib fantasies
Forget about Prada shoes and new hairdos
Cause nothing will matter if you don't strengthen up your gray matter for longevity of family
For a higher plane of thought, for your people will ensure a spot on the planet
For your children's, children to live in and have a place to sit down with food in their hands
Don't ever take that for granite

CLEO C. CONEY JR.

I'M ON THE OUTSIDE LOOKING OUT

People are trying to get into what I'm not a part of
I have my back turned against the crowd
I have my mind past the clouds
I can concern myself not of the popular choices
There's not one common interest belonging to the masses I miss
It's always been so since remembering far back in my youth
I'm on the outside looking out
Time passes on a separate plane of thought for my life
Far away from this place
I'm thinking about miles away from the furthest known spot
I'm contemplating a whole world not of this place
Worlds away from this place
A smoother, lovely place
Clear, crisp, blue, green, red, pristine
Full of a different focus
Focused full of a higher thought
My mind runs free here
My eyes see this place
My heart smiles for this place
There, love is placed on every, in every, and with every soul
I'm on the outside looking out
My back forms a wall
Keeping a line between this daily chase
The crowd's race, concerned about the now and the how's
All the while I'm separate of the known
My mind drifts alone
Passed all the skies our telescopes have known
Passed suns faint and small
I'm on the outside looking out
I dwell not of this big blue ball
The corners of my mind produce and project my happiest hours

Blonde

Blondes have more fun
That's the lie they preach
That's why sisters bleach
But once you go blonde you can always go back
When you remember that you're black
Caught up in so called celebrations of hair style and personal flair
These are the misconceptions that mislead minds with an appetite for the temporary
With a taste for the contemporary
Which promotes the use of horse and dead peoples follicles
Drenched in gold shafts

BULLETS RUN FAST

you say you run fast but bullets run faster
no time to duck and flex like in the matrix
no special effects can save your assets
you knew better than to mess with
what wasn't yours takes no detective
now the sweat, and the heart beat increase
like your chances
of dying from some smoking heat from inside some metal
ain't nothing for your family to laugh at
ain't no chance to get your life back
it was a fatal mistake to get wrapped up
in a game of life and death
a test you never passed at cause
you got caught up in the drama
and it will take more than you and a young boys momma
to lift the seal from a gangster's promise
the kiss of death for stealing paper
covered in headshots of dead presidents
one shot to your head and you're no longer a resident
the end result of a statement, to keep others from making
the same mistake in
dealing with the boys with high stakes and rolling merchandise
the kind you could of paid cash for if you had your life back
lots of drama in low places
life's unstable in high places
one thing for certain
the both include life races

BOBBING BAGS

Bobbing bags of saltwater carrying forged soil
Exterior colored in a varied mixture of browns, olives, and peaches
Intelligence measured only by the level of their midst
A comparison to none because aliens rarely visit
So we can only guess at how smart we are
Us and we
Just bobbing bags of saltwater carrying forged soil
A little bit of gray matter, a little bit of star dust

CLEO C. CONEY JR.

THE ALTERNATIVE

Not belonging to the jocks, nor finding kinship with family
An attempt to standout by a pierced, tattoo, and dyed rebellion
Takes place all over these states
The misfits gather in-groups, usually old parts of town
Some have artistic talents; others just want to belong to a group, any group
A group of pale skinned, thrift store bought, hapless souls try to stand apart
But in doing so, not one is singled out
Cause all share the same stylist, a passé' punk, retro today
An Edward Scissors hand groupie, singled out chumps
Tattered jeans, old Laura Ingle dresses with boots
Leather accessories, body jewelry, tongues pierced too
There's no more norm, because this group reinvents none
A meeting of the minds could easily analyze
These misfits dyed black, clothes tied dyed
Alternative to what is asked, since an alternative lifestyle is what claim is made
But somewhere I'd bet a bad hairdresser, and clothes stylist is getting paid!
Hugs from parents, lots of friends at school
Could end the cycle of jet black dyed hair dos

AND I SAW HER LAY

And I saw her lay
There on the bed before me still, quiet, yet hot a fire
Pillows sweetly, and gingerly keeping her head in constant comfort
She laid before my eyes in full bloom of beauty
Her small sleek sensuous feet hidden beneath covers that did not hide the waist,
Nor stomach, nor chest, nor neck of the beloved
There on that bed before me with eyes closed, and mind adrift in sleep
She lay like a mountain pool of fresh pure water,
Not worried by pebble, nor wind, nor creature therein, but still as steel, yet softer than butter
Her black hair looked satin smooth about her brow
It curled and danced down across her face of ledgen, skin like pure gold
On the bed before me was the woman I had prayed for,
The woman that perfectly fit every dream and fantasy detail stored in my minds safe
Her breathing was like music to my ears, soft short sure breaths
Her lips beckoned mine, yet I dared not taste of that strawberry honey until she ask of me
Her lovely hands perfectly balanced and caring
And I saw her lay
There on that bed before me in a room only enlivened by the faint voices leaving a television speaker
A huge storm crashed about my chest, and head
I was the only one who knew of it, I was the only one who felt the lightning strike
It's funny how comforting that storm was in that brief span of moments,
In the presence of the beloved
Nothing else mattered in that short span of moments,
In the presence of the beloved
Nothing else on earth mattered in that short time spent together yet apart

CLEO C. CONEY JR.

I longed to stroke her hair and lay with her like spoons stacked
To wake in the presence of her light would forever fill my life's voids
And she lay before me in full eye dripping view, as I always imagined she would appear to me
Body snaked to the side with her head straight, with curves, curves, and more curves
Venus must be green with envy, and cupid must be getting paid,
Because on the bed before me, my destiny is in the flesh
The future begins through this woman, this I cannot deny
This thing that hits you from the blindside, can't be predicted, nor foretold
In this woman's hands, my heart she holds

EYES OPENED

Hell fell over my head like snowflakes
My sunshine had vanished and no longer rose or set on my planet
So many contemplations filled my swollen head
Like a bag full of bowling balls my heart hung low to the ground
Love, which had seemed dream like had been snatched from me as easy as turning a lamp off
Cold and ashy from the lack of sunshine
A future facing a dead-end alley full of urine and broken glass
What kind of man could I of been?
What kind of man was I before?
I had abandoned my senses and allowed blind passion,
And love to fool me into the unsafe arms of trust
Panic will turn into steel, and a once warm heart shall turn into concrete
It's the smiles of the soft pretty eyes that grab you
Then ship you off to slaughter
It is my own fault I'm sure, for I haven't learned to keep to myself yet
I am not supposed to go through this life with another
This realization is certain, and fixed

CLEO C. CONEY JR.

IN THE PRESENCE

Hurry sunbeam and light this brow
Rush, rush, rays of warmth and love and carry me away
As I close my eyes to wonder outside my shell
Closer still sweet, sweet, star above
Give me my fill, and cover me so there's no shadow
No cold darkness left for me to feel
Rise up and down on me
I shall not be a foot
I will be stationary in your presence
Enjoying the gift from up high
All around me tightly bind me like a Christmas package
So bright, so warm
Oh sunbeam, gather round
Slowly, surely, daily
Light my humble brow

A CHANGE

You can feel a change coming
That inner feeling of change about to take place
As the clouds go from white to gray
You'll always notice something
Deep inside you know it
It begins as a breeze as soft as cotton
On the horizon a storm is forming
It's only a matter of time
But change is coming
We all know it's gonna happen
We all have to endure this change upon us
You can feel a change coming
Just keep walking
The change to take place insures we accept our fate
As inhabitants of this vast blue space

THANKS

I'm standing tall through it all
I'm shinning through the mud on my face
I'm grinning though they don't want me to be able to show
I'm finding happiness in my sorrow
I'm filling the hole in my heart with hope
I'm meeting each blow as a challenge to look forward too
I'm getting up after every fall
I'm bending, but I will not break
I'm sure of my positive outcome
Because I know despite everything that has happened to me
It could have been worse
So my tears are those of joy
And how I remember each of my mother's lessons on character
And my father's instructions on self- help, and self- trust
I know I've been blessed
So I give thanks

THE DOLLS

Oh look at all these pretty faces
Beauty captured by the stroke of a brush
Porcelain and plastic shapes all in place
On my shelves they stay
In cases they wait
Holding on to their special spot
Some have smiles on face
Oh how each one has a name, and a date of their arrival
So lucky to be selected
Added to the family of dolls in wait
Cherished by so few
Those that understand not of what's great
But for the collector's intuition quality is understood
I gather the good
Silent little dolls of mine
Hold fast to your examples of grace
Beauty not affected by age, hair realistically sprouted forth
Oh my dolls
Oh my boys and girls
Lifeless, soulless, figurines
Individual versions of man's visions of beauty and grace

CLEO C. CONEY JR.

THE AIR

Take me to where youth is the air I breathe
Share with me your pains and glories
Deny me not what you ask of me
But take me to where youth is the air I breathe
Always shall I work to please?
All I ask is that you do the same for me
Together we will explore what the earth has to enjoy
Together the world has no corner we will not see
But take me to where youth is the air I breathe
From day one we will exchange apiece of our hearts and minds
From day one we will not let time enter our lungs
We shall remain young at heart
Because we will only exist where youth is the air that we breathe

PATH

These drops of water as loud as car crashes
Deep in my mind shock waves creating craters
No aspirin for my life's vibrations can stop the constant flow of the world's problems into my head
My world shared by the rest of us, but the perception of it all is through my eyes
Which have seen many a glory
Life is full of different stories
They add up on my calculator making sense out of the sum of experiences I've been through
Can I start with you baby boo?
All a glow but in black and white
The moon shines right through these blinds
Bleeding away all of the earth's colors this night of each other
Safely in your arms I'm cradled, thrusting inside like no other
My heart is pounding, the end is in sight, but I'm all up in this love tonight
Sweet and sour, our love was like late night Chinese take out
Tastes good, fills you up for a while, but the hunger still cry's out
I reminisce about you boo, but it's just one story on my path, life's trail another tale to tell
Damn! I wanna yell!
My feet hurt because of the miles, but when I look back my heart smiles
I wish I could share in 3-D what good things have happened in my life
I wish you could see what I went through some nights
I'm on my path
Red glowing lights, a dance floor is flooded with these lights, I turned it out one night
Me and my "Self", she knows the drill, first name_____, last name _____
The second story on my life's path, for three years she shared laughs
On the dance floor we met, she would dance until she slept

She was sensitive, she gave me knowledge of self, her sister caught us one day upstairs
Almost wed, but my mind young in focus, missed this bus that drove the right way
No order to these stories anyway, I'll mix and match the delivery
It's written as my mind regurgitates flashbacks
Things that have happened to me on my life's path, life's trail, another tale to tell
Damn! I wanna yell!
Oh, how I was interrupted by Roxanne, and oh, it was she and her friend that took advantage of a young Blackman
A Caucasian Hispanic combination to bring a man's fantasy in focus
No prior warning, like a Pearl Harbor attack!
No man was ready, a brunette and blonde blitzkrieg all out
My plane caught fire, but I didn't bail out
I had no chance for escape, not that I'd run, for curiosity had the best of my senses
I followed they led
Music playing in the background, slides shown on the wall, mirror images in front of me repeated what I'd seen flash on the wall
Incredible, a spectacle
We were supposed to go out dancing the three of us; scared I was of the lust
I almost choked in disbelief of what these two women could do to a man from his head to his feet
Just one story on my life's path, life's trail another tale to tell
Damn! I wanna yell!
She was supposed to manage my supposed talent
Small time modeling she helped me out
But I ended up helpless in her presence; she owned the keys to my weakness
Step by step from a crawl to a walk
The way a woman teaches a man about the possibilities
About the shapes and what's in, about the textures and smells
She captured my youth's essence, turned me upside down, sometimes I cried out
Late night conversations, she held an all night love lab
I was the only student in her classes; she tried to turn me out

Just one story on my life's path, life's trail, another tale to tell
Damn! I wanna yell!
No order to these stories anyway, I'll mix and match the delivery
It's written as my mind regurgitates flashbacks
Did I ever panic in the church parking lot? I think so, but we couldn't think of a safer spot
Too young to have a place, no over night "no- tell" stay
Her parents I did not meet, my parents let her put up her feet and make herself at home
We met in school were we concentrated on college earth science
She concentrated on me like a repairman on an appliance
Great vibes between us two, for years we snuck around, sometimes in public and between relationships
We counted on each other like pacifiers and babies, a magnetism which last through this day
We call long distance and reminisce, talk about the past, take our time just saying hey
Just one story on my life's path, life's trail, another tale to tell
Damn! I wanna yell!
So many unspoken memories ink won't catch some of these, but they remain in tack
No portion escapes through my lips movement, just these few tales from my life's path

CLEO C. CONEY JR.

CONSPICUOUS CONSUMPTION

Conspicuous consumption? Ya'll, can't be talking about me
I need the things I buy, I don't even return the wrong size
You know I've got to have the best
Rolexes for my pets, including diamonds for my bird's nest
People dream about how I live
Platinum cards, charging cribs and cars
Each outfit I wear has a matching ride
Each car has it's own garage
Tonight my ride comes from garage number fifty-five
Conspicuous consumption? You've made the wrong assumption
Fendi, Gucci, Dolce, and Donna all live in my closet on the Westside
Don't try to battle, cause in my eastside it's loaded down
Count'em, three hundred and sixty five ways to counter
The weather, an event, or party, I've got something to wear that'll cut the mustard
Doesn't matter how many black slacks I already own
Cause there's a pair that'll work which will soon be in my home
I'm dripping with so many diamonds people keep throwing me towels
But I never sweat, cause my Bentley's A/C is kicking all day long with the fan at top speed
Roof down? Yeah, that's just how it be
A ghetto CEO maybe, conspicuous consumption I think not
Registers can't count as high as my charge limits
Let me take my dog for a walk, my poodle keeps a fresh weave cause cuts on pets are played out
She has a twenty four karat gold manicure, pedicure, hell, it's the whole set
Conspicuous consumption? Who me? Please
I don't have time for details, too busy creating bills which I pay to zero dollars every thirty days
My underwear runs five hundred and fifty per day top and bottom
I keep my hair comb in a glass case
My large screen TV would take up your whole place
What I want is what I need, what I need is too cheap to please

My only daily discussion is with myself about charging, and on which card
You'll never see me wear the same clothes twice in the same city
That's why I like to travel, but my favorite thing is to make the competition unravel
When they see me chilling like double "o" seven on her majesty's side
It's all they can do to keep up with my stride

CLEO C. CONEY JR.

New Cherry Blossom Dew

Perfume varieties dancing in my head
New cherry blossom dew
These are the moods of my vision
As my senses take in the multiplicity of eastern female youth
All the world can agree
An Asian beauty blends right into your, to my background
With flair they grace us with their faithfulness to trend, to tradition
Faithfulness to the men lucky enough to share their space
New cherry blossom dew
GOD blessed them when the pot of mixtures of men were poured into the land
New cherry blossom dew
Misty, soft, and silky sweet
Behold the balance of beauty from Asia's fruit
Blessed shall you be, when in the company of
New cherry blossom dew

AMBIENT ECHOES

THE WORLD GOES CRUNCH

Ma disbelief in a situation, started without no reservation
Pointing out those limitations
I'd be a relic to tell it, cause it happens to brothers all over the globe
While they claim you in the ranks, behind your back they claim you stank
And not one of em's on your side
Can it be the politics brought on by not owning shit?
Or could it be a reflection inside the individuals heart ticks?
May I hold firm to my folk's teachings
Let my skin be apart of no bleaching
I'm a man and I'm a tell it, you can't hold me my mind is swelling
Each day that passes I'm trying to pull up these bootstraps, but they be broken
My boots where used before my folks owned them
I can't watch my television, hidden messages in my play station
Got me spending on more games and playthings
All day long I watch my credit; you need it when you least expect it
But how long will these games go on?
I'm feeling like I'm trapped on an island, ship wrecked and I can't get my feet wet
What's the real reason my peoples be bleeding?
Why can't we just focus like a camera lens on a subject?
News bulletin, a church is on fire, and a group of people killed themselves hoping on a comet their souls would fly
So much trouble all around, fighting, and killing, but living on the same ground
Life is hell even on my memories, cause I can't reach back and enjoy them times again
See I'm getting older, but the world gets smaller
I'm wiser now, but it doesn't seem to matter
Young ladies no longer cook, young men can't even read a book
Technology has us going back
We refuse to think, letting machines do that
Everyone's wearing Hilfiger,

but he'll figure how to keep all your cash
Eighty-dollar jeans ain't worth that
I'm packing knowledge in my head like a gun, cause I don't trust living with metal
I don't want to shoot anyone
I'll aim with my minds bronze, worst-case scenario I'll run
To this day my momma's number one
I want to create and get paid in cash,
but I shouldn't focus on money
My life's worth more than that
But for my folks I want to build a huge home
While the world flexes, trying to hold me back, at work I'm pulling knives out my back
The OK corral keeps it simple, hold the beef, feed'em, breed'em, then your whole family eats
This rat race got my whole outlook focused on the cheese; this world has me saying please
Keep it simple, enjoy each day of life, help the youth straighten out before civilization passes out
Machines taking over,
terminators guns be smoking just like in T-2
But credit is the bullet, cash money the gunpowder
I can feel the world changing, I hope it gets better; maybe I'll unplug some of this stuff, or start an electrical fire
Stay strong in mind and body; always watch your back,
Don't be a deleted file on a banks program
Can you hear me?

THE EXOTIC

Young and tender just like fresh lambs fed milk
Strength measured in degrees of looks
They chase the almighty dollar
Getting men to holler at how tight or round
These smiles grow like loafs in ovens
For some this is heaven
No questions asked, for you they will dance
A two for one gets your wallet undone
All walks, all talks, from every direction
They are the sweets for the eyes saliva that drips in anticipation of fallen clothes
Eyes full but hearts empty
A rainbow of lights flicker as the watchers fulfill their task
A dollar in each garter to get things started
Every view the same yet different
Yet no eyes unglued
Here the spirits run free but the souls are cold
For centuries men have gathered to watch God's girls partly clothed
No reason as each woman's potential is contemplated to quench loins thirst
Man's weakness for the soft, sweet, and nice
Continues in this place tonight

CLEO C. CONEY JR.

GENIE

To the lovely genie in my life
Who doust grant me things I like
To par-take in a dinner night
An intimate setting to get things right
To the lovely genie in my life
With jet black hair that shines in the moon light
I thank you for the other night
Now I know you by name
You lovely genie in my life
Yes the company of you gets me right
Sets my heart a flutter
Wildly beating to the instructions of your smile
Your eyes so bright
Yes you are the lovely genie in my life
Named after the month of my birth
With matching gaps in our teeth
You've been selected prior to your arrival here in this place
To be the lovely genie in my life

THE GOOD OLE' DAYS

early in the morning it sometimes wakes me
slowly it calls to me
I try to ignore those tempting smells
which drift so effortlessly from my mother's kitchen where my pops is working his timeless magic
the sounds of the spoon being knocked on the inside of the grits pot after they've been stirred
in combination with the soft crackling sounds of the fresh mullet fillets in hot oil
my mother calls out to me, "sport!", get up!
followed by my sister's yell's, "Mang!", you heard momma call you, get up now
I have no reason to lie any longer; my stomach has already begun to get restless as it contemplates the Saturday morning inevitable southern styled breakfast, gulf coast fish and grits!!
yes lord, it doesn't get any better than this
but it's really not until you miss those hot fish breakfast's your folks prepared for you, that you really see the value in them
one must always enjoy the moment
because in that moment of tastes, family, and love
you are in the best times of your life
so don't let them go by too fast
Sit back and eat that fish slow

CLEO C. CONEY JR.

About The Author

Character is molded from lessons learned at a young age, "Ambient Echoes" a reflection on the classic spanking is just a glimpse at the character molding method that the author went through growing up. A hilariously funny, yet supportive look at a parents right to utilize the almighty spanking during child behavior modification. The author's butt remembers it well and now you too can reminisce about the good-ole days when the butt whooping was common practice.

A poet with a minds eye to observe many flavors of life, these selections provide something for every level of reader to taste. You'll marvel in the diversity of thought as he takes you deep inside his heart and head. From his observations of babies being "Little Clean Slates", to the depths of despair in "The Forgotten".

You'll know true joy in "Green", and true terror in "The Lie". With in these abstract thoughts emotions take a tangible form, emanating from the center of the author's soul. Enjoy.

Printed in the United States
6734